UNIMAGINED ODDS

By Marvin Alexander Ford

For permission requests, write to the publisher, addressed "Attention: Permissions Coordinator," at the address below. Amazon Book Publishing Center 420 Terry Ave N, Seattle, Washington, 98109, U.S.A

The opinions expressed by the Author are not necessarily those held by Amazon Book Publishing Center.

Ordering Information: Quantity sales and special discounts are available on quantity purchases by corporations, associations, and others. For details, contact the publisher at info@amazonbookpublishingcenter.com.

The information contained within this book is strictly for informational purposes.

The material may include information, products, or services by third parties. As such, the Author and Publisher do not assume responsibility or liability for any third-party material or opinions. The publisher is not responsible for websites (or their content) that are not owned by the publisher. Readers are advised to do their own due diligence when it comes to making decisions.

Amazon Book Publishing Center works with authors, and aspiring authors, who have a story to tell and a brand to build. Do you have a book idea you would like us to consider publishing? Please visit AmazonBookPublishingCenter.com for more information.

THANKYOU FOR HELPING

I would like to thank my writers' group at Sunriver for answering my questions and giving advice and input for my book.
This group helped organize my ideas.

I would also like to thank Jackie McFadden for all her support and feedback on the book.

Thank you to my son Timothy Alexander for the front cover of the book. Thank you to Paulina Tapia for helping edit my rough draft.

Finally, I would like to thank my wonderful wife, Claudia Alexander, for putting up with me and keeping me level-headed and focused.

DEDICATIONS

Unimagined odds

By Marvin Alexander Ford

In loving memory of my daughter Whitney Rey Alexander

RIP Sweetie Pum

INTRODUCTION

This story starts as a major event in my life ends. It is 1400 hours, and I have been told to report to my commanding officer. It is my exit interview as I prepare to be honorably discharged from the United States Navy. My decision to leave the Navy was made because I was engaged to be married. I told myself that I would never stay in the Navy if I was to get married. I wanted children soon after marriage, and I expected to be fully in their lives. Staying in the military would have made me, at times, miss large periods of time in my family's life. Therefore, Kelli and I decided that it would be in our best interest if I left the military. We wanted kids immediately so the both of us could have a lifestyle where both parents were home. We purchased a home prior to getting out of the US Navy. Everything was set up for us to start a family together. Although it was very tempting to stay in the military, our future children would be a bigger priority than remaining in the US Navy.

After our wedding and honeymoon in beautiful San Francisco, California. We moved into our freshly renovated condominium in Escondido, California. It was time to get started with our new family life. One day, I came home from work and was informed by Kelli that she did not want to have any pregnancies, deciding adoption was the way we would go. She went on to describe how we should adopt special needs babies. Her plan was to be a stay-at-home mom, therefore quitting her current job. I was floored and considered ending the marriage without delay. It was not a good moment in time for our young relationship at all. She stood her ground and was very content with this unilateral decision. We argued and were not talking very much at all. Then, one day, she showed me a picture of a set of twins, a boy and a girl. She informed me that she wanted us to be the foster parents for these twins. After much discussion, we decided to at least get qualified by taking a class to get CPR and First Aid certified. This took place at the local Red Cross center. By the time we had finished that class at the Red Cross center and had done the necessary mandatory classes at the center for foster children with special needs, I was warming up to it. In order to keep the peace, I went along with everything but let her know that I was still not all in yet. We got assigned a social worker to coordinate our orientation into being foster parents. Which included us safety-proofing our home and getting it inspected for approval. After all of this was completed, the Twin boy and girl were no longer available, bringing an end to a stressful couple of weeks.

Approximately a month later, Twin boys became available, and the big day came to go and meet these twins at our coordinator's office. We arrived on time with much anticipation, bottled up with raw nervousness. When they brought in the boys, they announced them as the twin boys. My reaction was immediate and filled with adrenaline. I fell in love with these little babies. They were still fighting off the effects of the drugs their birth mother consistently took during the pregnancy. It was explained to us that the birth mother was on many types of drugs and lots of alcohol throughout the entire pregnancy. It was also explained to us that just before birth, the birth mother was drinking heavily. It was as if she was trying to kill them. The birth mother had the twins successfully, thank God, and simply got up, leaving the babies in the hospital. In addition, none of the extended family wanted to take on the responsibility for the twin boys. In our minds, the boys were ours the minute we saw them. We got an invitation to visit the twins at their temporary foster home as often as possible. We started bonding with the boys quickly. They noticed us and reacted to our voices long before it was time to bring them home as foster kids. Later, that changed from foster to adoption.

I was honorably discharged from the United States Navy without much fanfare because the priority was to bring our baby boys home. With all of this going on, I entered the great unknown, "The Job Market." We decided early on that I would work and she would be a stay-at-home mom. So, I found a job through a temporary agency that would turn permanent after so many days. Shortly after I started working, Kelli quit her job, which meant that it was almost time to bring the twins to their new home. I worked odd hours, which would work out better when caring for the twins. Kelli would have the kids alone from 3 pm until 12 am. I would then relieve her so she could get some rest, and then we would tag team it. It was a great unknown, so any plan was better than no plan. We got to take the twins home for one night as a trial run, and it went well. Then, not long after that, we picked up the twins for good. The family who was fostering the boys were the most heartwarming people we had ever met. Years later, they ended up adopting twin girls. Tim and Terry must have left an impression on them.

Following the adoption of Timothy and Terrance, we threw a party, and it was an incredibly happy time for us. I do not regret anything that led to adopting the boys.

Three years later, we adopted their sister, Whitney. Timothy, Terrance, and Whitney all knew from very early on that they were adopted. We also shared all the information we had access to about their birth parents. They were never in the dark about their adoption, which I believe helped them cope with the fact that they were adopted. I made it a point never to lie to them, mainly because my past was filled with lies. We chose our children, and they were a blessing. I fell in love with them from the first moment I met them. It's been my pleasure to be their dad.

CHAPTER 1

THE FIRST YEAR

It is January 1991, and my Los Angeles Raiders are getting beaten badly by the Buffalo Bills. Suddenly, it is time to go and pick up our twin baby boys; they are 3 months old. We brought them home to Escondido, California, and we were so excited but scared all at the same time. The twins kept us on our toes, giving us a tremendous workout both mentally and physically for the first four months. We got accustomed to a routine that would help with sleep and got the hang of things quickly. Remember, these little ones needed extra assistance because of their underlying conditions due to being born positive for different substances due to their birth mother.

They had drugs & alcohol in Utero and after birth. Both babies were premature and weighed in at 3 and 4 lbs.

Almost immediately, Tim and Terry were diagnosed with Asthma. They would also end up with a plethora of allergies when checked. I personally devoted everything I had to prove every doctor who said that Tim and Terry would always be developmentally delayed wrong. Each child had a different diet. It was mainly because their allergies were not the same. This made it so we were more careful not to mix any of their baby formula. The older the boys got, the better they got, slowly but surely. There is a developmental chart that we obtained that followed our babies from birth to one year old. Yes, the twins were behind in many ways, but they were not as behind as they were perceived to be in my eyes. I was all in. Therefore, all negative comments irked me. All through their lives, someone doubted them in one way or another. Keeping in mind that Tim and Terry had many doctors' appointments, our calendar was always filled up with appointments daily.

As I author this book, I must take a moment to meditate every now and then. This is a very emotional part of the book for me.

I made sure to mentally stimulate the boys to help in ways that most normal babies would not need. I did this by reading books they loved excessively. I honestly believe that this had a profound positive effect on them later in their development. The drugs wreaked havoc on their sensitive little systems, such as the nervous system and their immune systems, to name a few. We gave them extra needed attention and extra hugs of love and affection. Tim and Terry reacted well, loving the attention. I would take them in their double stroller for very long walks, which would also settle them down. The effects of the drugs in their systems at such a vulnerable time as they developed in the birth mother's stomach were damaging. The stroller rides seemed to calm them down as they would look around at everything or just simply go to sleep. Our condominium had a pool located in a common area where everyone's front door faced the pool. This would one day become a problem once Tim and Terry started to walk, leading to us eventually having to move.

Since Tim and Terry were still in the foster-adopt children program, we were still subjected to inspection. I completely understood that it was for the safety of the twins. On one such inspection, they declared the pool situation too unsafe for Tim and Terry. They required that the pool be fenced in completely to be compliant. The Homeowner's Association

said no because they already had plans to remove the pool at some point. This troubling moment became the reality of us having to move.

At 6 months old, the twins would not go to sleep and had us struggling to get them to sleep. We talked with their Pediatrician and were told that we needed to slowly turn the table by not going into their room at the first sound of trouble (crying). The Pediatrician told us to start going in after 10 minutes the first time. Then, wait for 20 minutes before going in. Lastly, she instructed us to wait for 30 minutes before going in. We never made it to 40 minutes. I was surprised at how easily this worked. Anyway, the problem was solved after a few nights, and they started sleeping through the night.

Tim started walking at about 7 months old, while Terry took his time and started walking at around 1 year old. So, Tim would be flying around in his walker while Terry would be right behind in a fast crawl. That was very funny to witness. Terry fell down the stairs one day, landing at the bottom of the stairs and going straight into a crawl without ever crying. This scared the life out of us.

We decided to move to Mira Mesa, a suburban area of the city of San Diego, California. We found a nice home in a good part of Mira Mesa. But before we moved to our new home, the twins turned one year old. For Tim and Terry's first birthday party, they both got individual little birthday cakes. Terry ate most of his cake in complete satisfaction, while Tim got overwhelmed with everything and cried as he threw the cake everywhere. No one cared because it was a moment we all just embraced. It must have rubbed off on Tim because he cheered up, and all was grand. In the heat of the moment, I got a strong feeling of a

bonding moment. They say that blood is thicker than water, but at this very moment, I felt strong feelings of love. A feeling of love for them that was thicker than blood. They were mine, and I was theirs. The bond was set in stone, and I was 100% all in, without a doubt. That night, I knew they were mine, and my ambition in life was to make everything happen for them both to the best of my abilities. I would accomplish this in a positive way with no room for negativity. I also knew that I would challenge them and myself to go after all their dreams.

We moved into our new home in Mira Mesa with renewed energy to take on our new challenges. One such problem was tackling the speech impediment they had. The twins were developmentally delayed in speech and some motor skills. In between all the different developmentary type therapies they had, we constantly had to work with the twins at home. Lucky for us, Tim and Terry were willing participants in this trying process. With the boys cooperating with this process, it made everything a lot easier. Slowly, the boys would make noticeable progress. I introduced reading to the boys at a very early stage of their development. I wanted them to know the importance of reading. I read to them and had the audiobooks played for them. We would read to them constantly as well as play many singing games like "Old McDonald had a farm" and others. My favorite singing game was, "Itsy Bitsy Spider went up the waterspout, down came the rain and washed the spider out, up came the sun and dried up all the rain, now the itsy-bitsy spider went up the spout again." They absolutely loved it; this brought a lot of joy to my heart.

The first year after moving, as the twins were almost two, they experienced many illnesses, mainly Asthma. This resulted in the twins being required to take treatments with a machine called the Nebulizer.

It was not much fun for the twins to have to sit still during these sessions.

I'm very proud of my little guys and how they persevered through all of that with little to no fuss. Terry was hospitalized for several days due to an Asthma issue. It was a scary time for us all. We never left the hospital once during his stay. I prayed a lot during that time, with real concern. Terry reacted well to treatment and got better. It was our first crisis, with more to come in the future.

Right about this time, the twins turned eighteen months old, and punishment came into effect. What an experience that was. There were two methods we used: timeout (had a special chair for this) and go to your room. It got to a point where I had to start videotaping them while they were on timeout. I did this to start an honor system to build trust and obedience. Every time someone did something bad, we all looked at the video and corrected the problem. Once, while being videotaped on timeout, Tim was so angry he decided to throw his shoes at the video camera. The look on his face when I reprimanded him was shock and amazement (Busted). I showed him the video of him throwing his shoes at the camera. After that, to my knowledge, I never knew Tim or Terry to do that again. Yes, Terry had to sit through all of it.

The Twins' first real trip was exciting for all of us. We entered the terrible twos in September, but the twins were doing great. We were off to Sacramento, California. It was to celebrate Thanksgiving Day at Kelli's sister's home. The twins got plenty of attention from everyone. They were like Rock stars and were eating it all up. The first night at Kelli's sisters' home, all the fun started at bedtime for the twins. Keep in mind that the boys are wired after getting a ton of attention all day. The bedtime routine went without a problem, or so I thought. I read to them after they brushed the few teeth they had. The teeth brushing came with a song, of course. Here it is;

"It's time for Timothy and Terrance to brush their teeth so they can be very CLEAN! That's why we brush our teeth so they can be very WHITE! That's why we brush brush brush brush brush brush brush brush brush, and we brush...etc."

Until the boys erupt in laughter. Probably not a good thing when it is time for the little ones to be calm enough to fall asleep for the night. Then, it was time to settle them down and get them in bed for Dad to read them to sleep. Baths done, book reading done, teeth brushing done, and mission complete. Now it's time for their lullaby music, hugs, and prayers. I get up to leave, and all I feel is lots of love for these two little boys. I tell them that I love them after kisses and leave the room. I do not know why, but I really miss those moments with them. They finally fell asleep after my third bed check, or so I believed. About two hours later, I decided to go and check on them. I open the door, and there is a party going on inside. They have all the clothes out of the dresser drawers. Everything is spread all over the room. The sheets and blankets are also on the massive pile of stuff on the floor. Everyone came running into the room and were astonished at the spectacle in front of them. The twins froze like criminals caught in the act of a crime. I had to almost bite a hole in my lip not to laugh. When they saw that I was not angry, they relaxed and even laughed. We all ended up in some form of laughter.

CHAPTER 2

THE SECOND YEAR

Once we decided to take the twins to a restaurant, it was during their Terrible 2's. Tim decided that he was going to misbehave. I gave him two chances to stop, but he decided to continue and see just how far I would go. For the first time (not the last time), I gave him an ultimatum. Tim did it again, so I got up and picked him up to go to the car, just like I said I would do. To act right or be removed from the table and placed in the car with me. This, of course, meant that I would have to end my meal. Because of his behavior, we had to wait in the car for Kelli and Terry to finish. The look on his face was total disbelief. The boys found out early that if Dad said something, he meant it... literally.

Trip number two was to visit Kelli's father in Orlando, Florida. It is the first time Tim and Terry met their grandfather. They are two years old and in total terrible twos mode. Our second scary moment also involved Terry in their grandfather's pool. Being the over-protector I am, I was always near them. Being near the kids was second nature to me, no matter what. I was on high alert being around a swimming pool. On this day, we were enjoying the pool with the twins. And we decided that it was time to get out because of nap time for the little ones. We removed all the floatation gear from the boys to dry them with towels. Then, out of nowhere, Terry falls into the pool by accident. Without hesitation, I was in the water, pulling my son out. It happened so quickly; he never had a chance to breathe in any water, but it scared me to death. I must have hugged him and his brother as often as I could for the rest of the day.

"The garage sales escapades" became a weekly experience for the kids and us. Something unique came from these garage sales that was unexpected. It was surprising to us in this sense...Kids are unpredictable. Throughout the years, and especially during the holidays, Tim and Terry received nice gifts, but this garage sale experience was about to blow all of that up. We started going every weekend to garage sales and buying old toys that the twins picked out. The thing is, they started to prefer playing only with these old, cheap, beat-up garage sale toys. They no longer wanted anything to do with the expensive toys they had.

On one occasion, their aunt Kassi and her boyfriend Allen built the twins a playhouse out of cardboard and painted it blue. They absolutely loved it. How they played together was so wonderful to see. I got them a plastic bat and a ball to play baseball. To my surprise, the boys were particularly good at it. So good, in fact, they were hitting the ball over the fence a lot. I had to move them over to the field next to our home, where the older kids played. The older kids would ask me how old my sons were, and I would tell them. They would then look at them in amazement. While they were only two years old, I already had visions of Tim and Terry playing little league baseball when they got older. Already knew that the twins would be able to bypass T-ball (hitting a baseball off a batting tee). I also knew this because I was pitching to them underhand, and they to each other.

Even with all the positive strides the twins were making, there were still a lot of up-and-down moments. One of those was their delayed speech development as it pertains to their age group. On the other hand, the boys' motor skills advanced quicker than was projected by doctors and other professionals. We still had an exceedingly long road in front of us.

I had to work and bring home the money. Kelli did a wonderful job keeping up with every single appointment. The twins needed to work on their motor skills since they were hypertonic (Stiff muscles that resulted from the drugs their birth mother took during the pregnancy). We worked with the boys at home doing an assortment of different exercises the doctor recommended to loosen their muscles, as well as memory games and activities to improve their intellect. We did these in order to bring them as close to normal or even close to their age group as much as possible. I remember bringing the boys to speech therapy and watching them during their sessions. I would try to help them get to the proper pronunciation by reading to them and correcting them a little bit. Turns out all the therapy was successful; I was proud of the boys every time they pronounced a word properly.

The big day was upon us. It was time to follow through with the adoption of Tim and Terry. What an exciting time it was. The anticipation that the day had finally come was overwhelming. We loved the boys with all our hearts. I genuinely believe this was all meant to be, but I did not know if this was the truth. It felt like our paths crossing with these incredible little boys was nothing short of destiny. There we were, sitting with our coordinator and the boys on each of our laps. Facing the judge as he explained the process that was about to happen. I was emotional about how far we had come, and even though the boys already called me dad, after today, it was official. I remember sitting there feeling so fortunate to be in that courtroom at that moment, and it was monumental. Tim and Terry seem to be excited, just as we were all at this monumental event in all our lives. I still remember wearing a brown suit with my 90s-style haircut (the kid-n-play box cut). It all became real when the judge pronounced us the legal parents of Timothy Alexander and Terrance Alexander. The adoption celebration was a blur to me since my

emotions were high, and I was a new father. I was all in. I truly did devote my life to the boys. I would protect them at all costs and by any means necessary. I made them priority number one over even my own wants and needs. The first foster family and home, Tim and Terry, had had our backs throughout the entire process. Peggy came to the adoption celebration that evening with her husband and youngest daughter. They are nice and decent people who I really appreciate wholeheartedly for all their support. I will never forget becoming the twins' father. It was such a special moment in my life. A special night it was, especially when it was time to prepare the boys for bed that night. I sang to them a special song that I wrote just for them:

"The first time we met and fell in love, the first time, and we fell in love."

"The first time I looked into your eyes, I cried. Do you remember the first time we met and fell in love, the first time and we fell in love."

As I wrote this song, and especially when I sang it to my boys, my eyes would tear up because of the difference these two boys have made in my life. From that moment and beyond, we were solidified as fathers and sons. I wanted to promise them that I would always be there for them and do the right thing. I understood that I was now their role model and that humongous responsibility now landed on my shoulders. I was prepared to take that challenge on.

One day, my next-door neighbor called to inform me that Tim and Terry had thrown all their garage sale toys over the fence into their yard. So, I decided that this would be a good opportunity to teach the twins a

good lesson, the first of many natural consequences. A lesson on how their father would be parenting them, remember they are still two years of age at this time. I brought the twins over to the neighbor's backyard and explained to them that they needed to return their toys back into our yard. The kids are so great, in my opinion. They returned every toy to our own yard just as I instructed them to and with great enthusiasm. When we returned to our backyard, I informed them that they were not to throw their toys over the fence again. They both acknowledged that they understood that if they did throw their toys over the fence, they would not get them back. Well, they did it again, just like I knew they would. True to form, I was true to my word, and they did not get the toys back. The pain set in quickly as the meaning of disciplinary action set in. I got rid of the toys, so they had to accumulate more garage sale toys in a hard, time-consuming way. The boys learned a valuable lesson that day: that consequences will happen when they do something they were told not to do. Tim and Terry learned what natural consequences meant very early in life. Disciplinary events were calm and not so much dished out in anger at all. I would give them alternatives, and they could choose to do what is said or stop doing something I told them not to do. This type of discipline happened later when they were much older. Most of the punishments that happened at this early age were time out, being sent to their rooms (mostly for Tantrums) or simple redirects.

The next event in our world was about to happen, and it was a big one. Kelli told me one day that she wanted to adopt another child. This time, she wanted a girl. A baby girl and, of course, special needs like our twin boys, which did not go over well with me at all. I had major concerns since we had a lot going on with our twin boys. Think about it: normal twins that are not developmentally delayed or with all their health problems are still a lot, and I did not want our boys to be neglected by the new baby.

We decided to go through with it after a lot of hesitation and many lengthy discussions. I did not want our boys to be deprived in any way. Kelli assured me that would never happen. So, we contacted the same foster adoption program in San Diego, California. Then, we set it up to visit a three-month-old baby girl. She was just getting over having Hepatitis C and was born positive for multiple substances from her drug-addicted birth mother.

We arrived at the foster home in National City, California. One look at this little innocent baby, and I/we were hooked. Each time we visited, our bond got stronger with her. It was almost as if we were meant to be. I did not like the area where our little future girl was, but we were focused and very patient. Especially since we had to make lots of plans, it was a logistical mess, but we got there before we brought her home for the first time. For the twins, we brought them home for one night as a trial run. I think there was so much to prepare for since when you have a pregnancy, you have months to prepare for the baby, but we only had mere days.

Our baby girl came home, and everyone was so happy for us. The first thing we did was give her a bath. Kelli's mother, Marlene and her younger sister, Kassi, were the ones who bathed her. I had twin duty, and that needed 100% of my attention. Our little girl was named Dolores prior to coming home with us. It was changed to Whitney. I chose this name due to my appreciation for the singer Whitney Huston. We wanted her to get used to her eventual name, which she would receive once the adoption was official, so we called her Whitney once she was home.

CHAPTER 3

THE THIRD YEAR

W hitney turned out to be almost no trouble at all. She was such a quiet baby and did not cry much at all. Tim and Terry loved their little sister. The boys are now three years old and making progress in their developmental stage, which was a challenging work in progress. They were still delayed compared to their normal three-year-old group, but Terry and Tim were improving steadily.

We found out the hard way that the twins had outgrown their baby beds. One day, it was nap time for the boys, and we put them down as usual, assuming that all was well. Within thirty minutes, I heard a noise coming from their bedroom. Upon further investigation, I realized that they were not sleeping, and I could hear them playing. When I opened the door to their room, chaos was in full gear. The boys were out of their beds and on the floor breaking snow globes. The very snow globes they received from their grandmother (Marlene). They used the toy hammers given to them as a gift from us at the time. As you may already know, these snow globes were made of glass, and when shaken, the artificial snow encased inside this round globe moved through the water inside it to simulate snow. Once I entered their room and saw what they were doing, I immediately went into safety mode. I told the boys to freeze and not move a muscle. My main concern was their safety, especially because of all the broken glass everywhere. They had broken glass all over the floor and all around and on them. I removed each boy and stripped them to make sure they were not injured. After all the mess was cleaned up and the carpet dried, I made sure no glass remained anywhere in the room. I put the twins back into their beds and told them to get out of their beds. This was done with

the sides completely raised to see how they were able to get out of the bed. They were able to get out of their beds with extreme ease. I Packed up all three kids and took off for a furniture store to purchase them safer beds.

Unexpected fun happened by mistake with one of the old mattresses from their old baby beds. After setting up the new beds, it was time to remove the old baby beds. In the process of doing just that, one of the mattresses ended up sliding to the bottom of the staircase. The next thing I knew, the twins were jumping from the stairs onto the mattress at the bottom. It scared us at first, but we realized it was okay. They would jump down on this mattress as if it were the most fun thing to ever have been invented. Watching them do this was exciting, especially with how much they loved it.

As a new family who was brought together and not in the traditional sense, it nevertheless had no effect on us. It was lots of love and a type of cohesiveness that was evident in all our interactions with each other and with others in our inner circle. My memories of this time period always bring a smile to my face. Yes, we did not have kids in the conventional sense by adding to the population, but these are still my kids. Each day was a bonding time for our family of five. I know it was evident how we raised the twin boys differently than we raised Whitney. Not so much now, but more and more differently the older the kids got. The results from this are almost visible on the horizon in our thinking. I am one to always look at the big picture, which is what I am explaining here.

A short trip to Seaport Village and Coronado Island in San Diego, California, has come. For most of the trip, Whitney slept in a baby carrier against my chest. We had a fun and exciting time walking around Seaport Village. Then, it was off to Coronado's North Island. We got to do a tour of one of the ships I served on while in the US Navy, The USS Constellation CV-64.

Kelli and I got our real estate licenses with the idea that we would work as a husband and wife-team. I remember pulling both boys around in their red wagon as I would hand out flyers to prospective real estate clients. It was a fun period because of all the time I had with the twins.

Babysitting problems came up one day while both Kelli and I were out doing our real estate duties at the office. Better Homes and Gardens reality was the office we operated out of. The babysitter called to tell me that Tim was having a tantrum and would not come out of his room. She informed me that Tim was underneath his bed and would not come out from under his bed. I told her that it was her lucky day. I told her to just tell him to come downstairs once he felt better. Sure, enough like clockwork, she called back, and all was fine. Tim came down and was in a better mood. I knew he would be fine because I had gone over their room with a fine-tooth comb...it was completely safe.

Soon after this, we went out and bought a new swing set. A swing set that was a little more expensive for us, but safety came first in my book. For a change of pace, I would give Kelli and our precious daughter some peace and quiet. I would often take both Tim and Terry to Balboa Park in San Diego, California. It was good for the boys to be able to run around without too many restrictions. For some odd reason, On the 4th of July, we got the wild idea to take the kids to see the fireworks near San Diego Bay.

We got front seats (perfect viewpoint). Then the fireworks started with a blast, of course. I think we were back in the car heading back home to Mira Mesa before the fireworks show was even over. The kids had a negative reaction and were not having it at all due to sensitivity to loud sounds, another effect of the drug exposure prior to birth.

The first camping trip was to William Heist campgrounds near Julian, California. It was a very good trip, as our children took to it well. Grandma Steward came out to surprise the kids (she spoiled the kids, which was always okay). We had no real problems except during the middle of the day because of the heat. We had purchased a new Dodge Caravan, which turned out to be perfect for our family transportation needs.

We decided to try our hand at having more foster kids, and before I knew it, it was a reality. I helped Kelli a lot, but she was rather good at it, and I was mainly watching our kids. For whatever reason, as quickly as it started, it was over as we reunited two babies back to their birth mothers. They had lost them at birth because of drug problems. Mickie and Promise are two of the sweetest little angels. All was gone except for a little boy a few years older than Tim and Terry. His name was Donte, and his sister would also end up with us for an abbreviated time. Donte had behavior problems and had once been left in a hotel room with his other siblings for days when he was only six years old. His birth mom still had visitation with him. I was tasked with the duty of facilitating the visitation between Donte and his mother. Donte seemed to do better behavior-wise the longer he stayed with us (as a foster child).

CHAPTER 4

THE FOURTH YEAR

The Head Start program began with Terry having no problems, just hoping right in as if he belonged. The only possible problem, I guess, was that Terry was a hugger. He would hug anyone, so of course, the first time in a class setting with kids around, Terry hugged all day. We got the advice to tell him to stop with the hugging. I thought it was petty, but then again, rules are meant to be followed. We worked on it, and he seemed to adjust to not hugging the other kids in his class. There were only a few times here and there when he forgot, but that was seldom. Tim, on the other hand, was a whole different story. He wanted no part of the Head Start program and made it known to everyone within earshot. I had to stay the first few days until Tim would allow me to leave. Every now and then, he would erupt into a full tantrum, which gradually went away with time. Eventually, the crying stopped, too.

This daycare incident was almost funny but still serious enough to show up and pick up the Twins as demanded by the daycare lady. As I explain what happens, it is okay with me if you laugh yourself to tears. I had to hold it while in front of the boys. In private, Kelli and I laughed to tears. It was a normal morning, except it was kind of cold for southern California. I got the kids fed breakfast, with both in good moods. They knew that they were going to daycare, so it was not a surprise. We arrived at the daycare, and I brought the boys inside to drop them off. Everything seemed well enough, so I took off to start my day. About thirty minutes later, I got a call from the daycare. This lady was crying on our phone call when she informed me that I had to pick up Tim and Terry because of an incident involving Tim. I asked her if the boys were all right, and she said yes, they were fine. Finally, she told me that she asked the boys to remove their jackets.

Terry took his jacket off and went back to playing with the other kids. Tim said that he was HOT! He got confused, meaning that he was cold. He wanted to keep his jacket on. Since he was saying he was hot instead of cold, the Lady decided to remove his jacket herself. When she started taking it off, Tim reached back and slapped her as hard as he could, according to the lady. She left his jacket on and called me immediately. When I arrived to pick up my twin boys, the lady told me that they were not welcome back. I truly believe that she had to have been rough with him, number one. Number two, I thought that she could have just let him keep his jacket on. I mean, like, what is that going to hurt? By the look of the slap mark on her face, I was lucky not to be getting sued, honestly. Her face on one side was beak red and bruised. To me, how can a 4-year old inflict that much bruising? Then again, Tim and his brother were hitting home runs with ease at two years old.

It's time to go camping again, but this time it will be a long trip. It was a camping trip combined with two-day passes to both Six Flags Magic Mountain and the water park. Kelli's sister and her boyfriend Gerry came with us. It was a nice trip for the kids and us for a change of pace. It was a camping trip that I felt the kids would remember, except Whitney. The kids were limited at the amusement park because they were not tall enough for most of the rides. However, with that being said, we found things for the kids to do. One such thing was a large slide that they played on a lot. Donte did not want to go down the slide, even though Tim and Terry were loving it. Gerry and I finally got Donte to go down the slide, and the yell he did was beyond funny. Donte yelled all the way down the slide with something sounding like Mommy! The Water Park was a hit with the kids and adults. Overall, it was a great trip for everyone. I enjoyed camping more than anything, especially since amusement parks with rides are not my idea of fun.

The start of the pottery business begins with high hopes. The name of our new business was A Unique Boutique. The business partners were Gerry, Kelli, Julie, Kassi, and me. It was a business that consisted of buying pottery from Tijuana, Mexico, and painting both the pottery and framed canvas pictures. We would load up my truck with the finished product, and then the kids and I would go to our rented area at Coby's swap meet in San Diego, California. I did not know it then, but this would all later end up going down in flames. A liquidation of the business and everyone would go their separate ways. This would lead to us moving again and uprooting the kids once again in the future.

We moved to a bigger home, along with Kelli's sister and boyfriend, Julie, the kids and me. This was a big home with five bedrooms, a swimming pool and a jacuzzi. I admit at first, I wanted nothing to do with this ideal, but the business was still afloat, and it had a pool. On the walk around with the landlord, Tim stepped on the soft cover of the jacuzzi and fell in completely. I do not even remember much, except in an instant, I had my son out very quickly. At some point unbeknownst to me, the house was determined to be haunted by ghosts, by Kelli and Kassi. I had never seen anything, and the kids had never seen anything either. Everyone wanted to move except for the kids and me, who were swimming in the pool just about every day. The plan was set to find another place to live. I had just gotten used to the house and did not understand what the problem was. I then started driving for an air freight trucking company for a friend of mine. Little did I know how I would really take to driving Trucks.

For a change of pace, we all went camping at the Indian Reservation's camping grounds on Palomar Mountain. I had no idea we would eventually be on this camping trip for two weeks. Gerry and I would go back to work and return on the weekends. When we got back, I decided to go to a trucking school to get my commercial driving license.

A few months later, the boys went to the desert off-road section of Glamis, California, for the first time. This was a haven for the dune sporting activities. The twins loved playing in the dunes, jumping off small dunes and landing in soft, puffy sand. We were invited by my lifelong friend Patrick. I marveled at the pure excitement that Tim and Terry were experiencing on this camping trip. To see how much they liked it made this a winning trip. I would make plans to do this again and bring Whitney with us. Donte missed out because of his visiting time with his birth mother. I could also see myself purchasing an ATV for myself and eventually one each for the twins.

One time on Halloween, I took Tim, Terry, and Donte to a haunted house. It was the first and last time I would wear makeup as Herman the Monster. Kassi did my makeup, and from everyone around me, I was told that it was an excellent makeup job. The kids told me I was scaring them, and I tried not to laugh aloud, but might have. Everything was going great until we came up to this haunted house. We debated on whether to enter the haunted house or not, but we finally decided to enter anyway. I tried to let the children know that it was all make-believe and nothing was real. I got some unsure looks back, but they all said okay and wanted to go inside. We entered the haunted house and did not get ten feet inside when the boys lost it with fright. They

wanted out of there now, but it was impossible because there were too many people behind us to turn back. They screamed it out the whole way through, with tears galore. I tried not to let the kids see me laughing, but it was tough. When we got out of there, I was relieved to see that my poor kids were not traumatized.

CHAPTER 5

THE FIFTH YEAR

Kindergarten half-day classes began for Tim and Terry without any problems. Whitney was still at home with Kelli, and Donte was entering the second grade. I wanted to hold the twins back one year from starting Kindergarten because they were still delayed in their development. Kelli fought me on this and wanted them to attend anyway to stay on schedule. I was worried about the regular elementary schools in the future and if they would be ready. I hoped I was wrong, but we would find out.

I stumbled upon something that would bring the twins and their sister joy for years to come. It was the big wheel toy (a big wheel in front with two smaller wheels in the back) that brought my kids so much joy. Early on, they would only ride on the sidewalk in front of our so-called haunted home. I would push Tim and Terry up and down the sidewalk for hours. Another thing the twins and I did was throw rocks. Yes, plain old rocks, what seemed like for hours at a time.

Trucking school started and ended in no time at all. I then decided to go with an over-the-road company out of Phoenix, Arizona. While I hated leaving my kids, I had to go over the road in order to obtain experience. I only stayed at this job for three months. I was back home to work locally and be at home daily. The twins were only five years old at this time and needed their father at home.

Everyone moved out of the so-called haunted house, leaving only my family there. Kassi and Gerry moved to Escondido while Julie found a place in San Diego. We had the house to ourselves until it would be time for us to also find a place to move to.

I decided to go wash the Van at the carwash, and the twins wanted to come with me, so off we went to the car wash in good spirits. Got in line at the drive-through car wash, and all was good. The very moment we started traveling through this carwash, Bam! The washing started with brushes spinning and water spraying against the glass, and the noise was too much for Tim and Terry. Both boys tried to hide under the bench seating in the

Van. I had never seen anything like it before. All I could do was try not to laugh out loud. They were in total distress and scared out of their wits. It reminded me of when I once took the twins to an Easter bunny, and they had a similar reaction. They cried on Santa's lap a year earlier, but only Tim tried to do a complete escape routine by running from Santa.

The three boys started this thing where there was a lot of rough play. Many times, ending in near-fighting situations. I had the perfect remedy to solve this problem all figured out. I went out and bought two sets of boxing gloves. Set up a perimeter (for safety) for a boxing ring. First up was Donte, who always picked on Terry and, of course, Tim. Donte beat up Terry good. Terry spent most of his time trying to grab instead of throwing punches and jabs.

What I did not expect was Tim's reaction to seeing his twin brother get a beat down. Then, it was time for Donte and Tim to go at it, with Tim visually being angry. Tim wasted no time by throwing a left cross straight onto Donte's nose, and that was the end (Tim was a southpaw while the other two boys were Right-handed). Tim, two years younger than Donte, beat him up and made a point not to mess with Terry again. Busted Donte's nose and caused him to cry like a baby. Tim stood over him and told him to leave his brother alone. I was amazed at how Tim took up for his brother like that, and it made me proud of him. From that day on, I never again had a problem with them fighting. Donte Definitely respected Tim from then on, for a good reason, too. This meant Donte would not touch Terry because of fear of retaliation from Tim.

The big move has come to fruition, and it was to a place far away called Valley Center, California. By this time, I was comfortable with my new job, and our finances were in good standing. I love being the breadwinner by having my woman be home full-time while I work. We moved to our new home with four acres of land. It turns out to be heaven for our three kids and Donte because there are so many things to do and the wide openness. The kids loved riding their Big Wheels down the many hills that surrounded our new home. Whitney was right there with the boys like a competitive rider. It was good to have something to take the place of the pool from our last home, which the kids enjoyed to the fullest. Just like these hills, they would swim each day. In fact, they all learn how to swim at the other home with the pool. They adjusted quickly to our new home and grew to love Valley Center, California.

New dogs, Bear and Smoky, whose names came from my trucking career and occupation as a trucker (meaning Smoky Bear, the highway patrol). From this point on, the kids would always be around dogs. I grew up around dogs most of my childhood. In fact, my personal message to this book will be about my beginning and what shaped me into the man that I became. I must do this so it is understood what my ambition was all about. which is the fact that a little woman, my grandmother/mom, born in 1908, shaped me into the man I am today. Speaking of Bear and Smoky, "these fools" ran off one day and never came back. The kids asked if I would go after them, and I said no. They had it made in the shade but decided to leave on their own. I explained to them that one day, they, too, will decide to go off on their own when they become adults. I also told them that I would not try to stop them either because it would be their destiny. They looked at me as if they understood exactly what I was explaining to them. I know that it was my duty and responsibility to turn my boys into men (the opposite of males). Once they told me that they were men, I knew my job would have concluded.

Terry was the first to have a fishing experience with his uncle Gerry. The kid caught a fish and was hooked for life from that point on. I've never seen a kid more focused on fishing than Terry. I really enjoyed all his plans to become a professional fisherman. We found a camping ground with three lakes and decided to try camping there. Lilac Oaks camping grounds, as we arrived with as much gear as we could haul, it looked perfect. The kids got to ride their bikes, fish, and do many other things.

(I think it will be a good idea to add pictures to this book,which will help to enhance our story.)

CHAPTER 6

THE SIXTH YEAR

The summer has a lot of twists and turns, with exciting times as well as some dangerous and scary events. Overall, it would turn out to be an adventurous first summer at our new home in Valley Center. The kids had so much fun with four acres of property to do activities on. They would spend time in the Jacuzzi, bikes, big wheels, and who knows what else. I gave them a lot of information on how dangerous snakes, scorpions, spiders, and tarantulas were. Not to forget that the coyotes were also dangerous, and strangers were to never be trusted. Before Bear and Smoky ran away, I felt good having them watch over the kids. Two German Shepherd mutts mixed with who knows what. Sometimes, I would sit and just watch the kids running around, just being happy kids without a worry in the world. Every now and then, I would take them camping and fishing because it was such a great family bonding time. Tim and Terry were naturals at fishing, many times catching more fish than their father. That gave me so much joy to witness those instances with them. Whitney could care less about fishing, even though she was sort of a tomboy, but not completely. Donte just went through the motions but did have fun just being involved.

The big day was when I found a used basketball goal unit, complete with a backboard and stand, for sale. The kids were so excited when we got it home and all setup. Now, I must say that right about this time, I got into using the US Navy vocabulary. Later, it will come in handy for the twins. When we were putting this basketball goal back together, I used Navy lingo and basically continued for the remainder of their childhood. Tim was mechanically inclined and loved helping me out no matter how tough the task was. Terry was not into manual work of any kind and had no interest at all.

So, it was mostly Tim and I who put the basketball goal up together. We played basketball from that point on until Tim and Terry were grown up. We got a lot of use out of that old basketball goal. I do not believe any of the kids will ever forget that thing. Keeping on the Navy angle, I started implementing the five-minute shower requirement rule. Okay, I really did not stick to it being five exact minutes at first. The reason was to start working on their discipline. On laundry day, they were required to be involved, not actually washing and drying their clothes (that would come later), but involved they were. They learn little things like a little folding, but mostly putting the clothes away in their dresser drawers. Kelli put them all on a reward system using colored stars, with each colored star meaning various positions on the reward board.

Hell week happens when I am not at home. I was off driving over the road in a big truck, making the money. The first thing that happens is a snake of some sort (probably a rattlesnake) gets killed by the boys. Not only do they kill the snake, but they also shin the snake. Remember that Tim and Terry are only six years old at this time. Donte is eight, and Whitney is only three years old. I could not believe my ears when I found out about this extremely dangerous act. What saved them from the raft of Dad was that I also did the same thing when I was a kid back in Louisiana. It was a water moccasin, just as dangerous as the rattlesnake. They got a major amount of counseling, which is when the term "come to my office" was born. My office was the restroom, and the intent was to make it unpleasant. I would be on the toilet as I would give them counsel. They hated it so much that it was not needed much. It cut down on dangerous things to a sliver of what it was before.

The next incident to happen was too serious to just give a pass on. They (the three boys) made the unwise decision to steal a book of matches from the house. I say steal because they didn't ask and because they knew it was wrong. Starting a fire in southern California is a very serious thing to do and dangerous. The threat of wildfire is prevalent at about any time of year. There seem to always be drought conditions. Therefore, the seriousness of this act had to be a teachable moment. Kelli was able to extinguish the fire and gave me a full account in front of the guilty parties. I reprimanded them harshly because I wanted them to understand the seriousness of the situation. I had many talks about fires and matches, plus the dangers to property and how people could be killed. I got outside information and went over that with them, too. I believe this incident was a helpful learning opportunity with consequences that have stuck with them to this very day.

First-grade time for the twins, and the whole atmosphere in our home is upbeat. The school they were attending in Valley Center was set up with only two grades per building. The first and second grades were together and separate from the third and fourth grades. And so on, with the fifth and sixth grades being in a separate building also. The twins had come so far at this point, with their speech being almost normal and approaching their normal age group.

CHAPTER 7

THE SEVENTH YEAR

The kids took it rather well that Bear and Smoky had run away earlier this year. It took us a few months to get another dog. It was a black labrador, which we named Shadow. As I stated earlier, I grew up always having a dog myself. In my opinion, I believed that having a dog as a companion and playmate might help the twins. The kids became very close to our new dog, Shadow. While walking our dog one day, we all ended up goofing around under some rotted-out Avocado trees. There was a broken-off limb with part of it still attached. I got the wild idea to start trying to break off the rest of this limb. Finally, I told the kids to spread out knuckleheads. I got this. I pulled down on this rotted limb in a powerful way, causing the limb to break only about five inches on the end. Unfortunately, the rest of the limb produced such force that it connected with my chin. It literally lifted me off the ground and into the air, where I then ended up on my back. I almost lost consciousness as I had to really work on not passing out. I could see that the kids were very frightened, and they just stared at me in total disbelief. They looked up to me as if I were Superman, so this was surprising to them. The front of my work shirt was covered in blood from a cut on my chin where the limb struck me. I got up and pretended that I was fine even though I was not due to the fact that I almost blacked out. I never went to see a doctor, but I quite possibly could have had a concussion. I think from that point on, my kids really did see me as Superman.

The Disneyland trip was upon us, and to tell you the truth, it is not high on my list of fun places. The kids were so excited, and I could not mess that up for them.

I did tell them that the next time they went to Disneyland, they would be going on their own. Nevertheless, the trip was set, and we were going. We arrived the day before and stayed at a motel near Disneyland in Anaheim, California. All was going well until Terry had an Asthma attack. It got worse even though we had a special medication called Albuterol. Suddenly, the situation had become serious. Terry was having a lot of problems breathing. We loaded up and headed to the nearest hospital emergency room. They took him right in and gave him several types of medication that seemed to work almost immediately.

Terry recovered well enough not to have to be admitted to the hospital. I think staying in a cheap motel was probably what did our little guy in. Tim and Terry were both checked again for allergies, where they found multiple. One of them was dust mites, which is what that motel room probably had a lot of and is likely what set off Terry's Asthma.

Tim had two events that caused us to have to take him to Rady's Children's Hospital in San Diego, California. The three boys had the bright idea to ride on their skateboards in the seated position instead of standing on it, with no helmets on and even worse, they were riding downhill. Everything was fine when they were riding solo. At some point, Donte and Tim decided to ride together. Well, shortly after they did that, they crashed, and Donte ended up landing on top of Tim, causing his head to contact the pavement very hard. We immediately called the doctor and were told to bring Tim to Rady's Children's Hospital. The doctor also told us not to let him fall asleep at any time while in transit to the hospital. There was a possibility of a head/brain injury, especially since he was trying to sleep and was disoriented. We got Tim to the hospital, and thank goodness it was determined that he was fine. Afterward, I held lots of counseling sessions on everything to do with this incident.

The next situation with Tim was the day he ran through the cactus area and stepped on one barefoot. This cactus needle went in through the heel of his foot and out the side of his foot. Picture sticking an extra-long toothpick through the heel of your foot at an angle, with part of it still sticking out where it entered and part of it sticking out where it exited. We get the doctor and are simply told to do nothing. This was one of those instances where your body causes this foreign object to exit on its own. A few days later, it came out as we watched in amazement.

Approximately a month later was Tim and Terry's first experience playing live pitch baseball (coaches pitch). We get to the first practice, and Tim tells me that he does not want to play baseball. Everyone is arriving to practice, and here we are, on day one, having an issue. So, I told Tim that he would not have to play if he didn't like it after playing for a little while. He bought this and played from that point on for the next ten years. I was able to help coach their team and enjoyed experiencing this time immensely.

Another camping trip for the Alexanders after the twins' baseball season ended, which we all loved. It was a nice way to relax and have a change of pace while allowing the children to experience nature. Campfires were a major enjoyment for the kids, especially since I heavily regulated anything to do with fires at home. Anyways, the kids were allowed to play around the campfire in moderation and under heavy supervision. For the kids, it was all about roasting marshmallows for making S'mores and roasting hot-dogs. They made bread-baked pies right in the fire, too. We were careful in protecting the kids and ourselves from insects like mosquitoes, spiders, etc. They would run up the big hill and roll down it for hours. I can still hear their laughter and joyful little voices when I reminisce. All our camping trips bring back fond memories that will always be special to me.

The start of the second grade brought more excitement and made me happy to witness it first-hand. The twins were soon to be seven years old and still on the gradual pace of catching up to the proper development stage of children in their same age group. Shortly after school began, maybe a month or two into their school year. We were informed that the twins were diagnosed with ADHD (Attention-Deficit / Hyperactivity – Disorder). They explained that kids with attention issues cannot finish tasks, keep track of time, and have problems following directions. They also suffer from hyper-activity, meaning that they do not sit still, do not play quietly, and don't stay seated during class. When coupled with impulsiveness, they talked out of turn, had problems waiting in line, and would not wait for permission to use other children's things. We were not shocked but were concerned, especially when the recommendation suggested medication to solve/help the problem of Tim and Terry's alleged condition of ADHD. Eventually, both boys were put on the drug Ritalin, and before we knew it, they were experiencing side effects. Like when they would drink soda or eat candy, it would have a reverse effect on them. They had problems sleeping, which caused other issues which complicated the whole situation even more. So, Kelli and I decided to take them off Ritalin. We did a little research and found other ways to manage ADHD children in school (a different method of learning) without the use of medications. For instance, extra help in the classroom and learning at a different slower pace. Sometimes, they would have to be pulled out of class for one-on-one instruction. Personally, I am not a proponent of drugs for kids in general (in some cases, I know there is no alternative). I understand that there are some cases where drugs must be used, but the side effects I have seen in my twin boys were too much to allow it to continue.

CHAPTER 8

THE EIGHTH YEAR

Baseball time again, so I put Tim, Terry, and Donte through spring training. In other words, everything would be a different intensity compared to their level of play. They got a lot of batting practice with live pitching from Dad. At first, they got to learn how to catch fly balls as well as ground balls at normal levels, but then it quickly transitioned to a higher level. When they started playing, they were more advanced in the batter's box, meaning they did not fear being hit with the baseball. Keep in mind that I am six feet six inches. Nothing they would encounter from their opponents could ever compare to being pitched to by me. They could catch fly balls with confidence and without any fear. At tryouts, after a few weeks of working with them myself, they looked good. Incidentally, Donte misjudged a fly ball during tryouts and got hit in the nose. During the entire season, Donte never missed another fly ball after that mishap at tryouts. I was so proud of them for going through tough training with me without ever complaining, even though that would not have done them any good. They had respectable seasons except for Donte's hitting, which was a work in progress. Catching balls in the outfield came very easy for Donte. He was good at it. Tim and Terry were fairly good, with some good baseball skills.

The first of many camping trips with only the kids and I was during the early summer. I really look back at those times with lots of great memories. We pretty much went without all the rules we all adhered to when Kelli was with us in order to keep peace. This trip is when Kelli's sister's husband, Gerry, came along. It was a blast of fun. It was so relaxing for us and the kids. We ate when we were hungry and not at any precise time set. Meals were fun and not complicated. We

took one-third of the camping supplies with no complicated food items. We played with the kids when they wanted to without a set schedule to follow. On the first night out camping, we experienced a shorter time setting up camp. When the women were along with us, we were still expected to prepare a large meal, no matter what. Without the women, it was a bucket of fried chicken or bologna sandwiches. We also fished at night, a no-no with the women along on camping trips. We had so much fun with no stress. It was a stinker when it was time to pack it up for our trip back to reality (home).

Time for the first day of school, and as usual, all the kids were in great spirits. The Twins were headed to the third grade, Donte the fifth grade, and Whitney was just starting preschool. It was a big deal for my little girl. Terry came home one day without his jacket. When asked why, he explained that while on the school bus, his window was down, and his jacket flew out of the window. Picture this: all of us return to the scene of the crime to search for Terry's jacket. We never found it, but it was a memorable experience, nonetheless. Of course, this was another opportunity for a counseling moment for all three boys in my 'office.'

Later in this school year, another meeting with Tim and Terry's administrators was held on the subject of ADHD. After much debate, it was determined that Tim and Terry indeed needed help because they were behind in their schoolwork and studies. This wasn't a surprise to us because we, too, were seeing proof of this. An example of this was Terry racing through his homework to go play. Tim was having problems with math homework to the point where he was erasing so much when doing math homework that there would be holes all over his work. The boys were not at a point where the study material was too hard for them; it was that they needed a unique way of being taught. The end result was to put them on an ADHD medication called Wellbutrin, which seemed to work for them.

A little while after our meeting about their ADHD, Terry got suspended from school for a day. It began with a friend of Terry's, who was getting picked on. My son decided to take matters into his own hands. He picked up a wooden branch from under a tree and used it as a weapon. The kid (the bully) was bigger than Terry and his friend. So, Terry grabbed this tree branch and struck the bully kid on his leg extremely hard, as it was explained to me. Thank goodness we weren't sued over this incident. Terry was suspended and had to spend the day at home with Dad. For some reason, Terry thought this would be just another day at home from school. I can assure you that he quickly found out that it was not at all just another day. He ended up sleeping/laying on a cot on the floor of my bedroom as

I slept to get ready for work that night. Terry wanted no part of staying home from school after that. Not even when he was semi-sick, he would get upset if anyone even mentioned him staying home from school. Well, who would have ever known but my kids all had near-perfect school attendance records?

CHAPTER 9

THE NINTH YEAR

The big move was quickly upon us, and it was a major operation to pull this one off. The kids weren't all in on a move to Chicago, Illinois. Donte did not want to go at all, and I agreed with him. Kelli wanted him to come, so that thing went back and forth for a while before he changed his mind. We decided that I would drive the moving rental truck with Tim and Terry along with me. Whitney and Donte would fly with Kelli ahead of us. My very good friend Zack came out to help along with Gerry and another friend, Patrick. They helped us pack and load up the rental moving truck. I was so grateful for their help, plus Kelli's sister (Kassi) was also a big help. We stopped in Las Vegas, Nevada, Salt Lake City, Utah, and Galesburg, Illinois, for a total of a two-and-a-half-day trip to our new home in Arlington Heights, Illinois. The big thing I took from this very long drive was how the twins enjoyed the entire trip. They behaved so well and listened to me extremely well. They were simply very polite the whole trip, and I am very proud of these two little guys.

Chores became a regular thing in my kid's life right about this time period. First up were simple things like picking up in your rooms. I'm ex-Navy, so there were a lot of odd jobs I would have them do. I would judge their attitudes closely just in case we needed a counseling session or not. Next up was bagging leaves in paper bags, and then on trash day, it was staging time, so the leaves bags would be picked up. Next up, snow shoveling to clear our driveway and sidewalk. One morning, when it was very cold after snowing the night before, I had Tim and Terry join me outside to shovel the snow. It was minus nine degrees and very cold. I had the boys shovel a little, then sent them both back inside to warm up. The lesson for them to learn was that no matter how cold it was, it was not a good enough excuse to get out of chores. I wanted them to learn that, as a man, you cannot use excuses when you are the head of the household. I would tell them this from that day until they left home for good. They found out the hard way many times after this day just how serious I was when I would say, "I don't accept excuses, even if it was a good one." I never gave idle threats to them, meaning if I said this would happen and they disobeyed, it happened without any variations.

It's time for Little League baseball tryouts in a different state (Illinois). These baseball tryouts were different from what we were accustomed to in California. What they did was grade all the players' skill levels and abilities. Then, each team had to pick a player from each skill level to make sure no super team would emerge. Each team ended up being as close to me as I had ever seen before. I really loved this system, for the kid's sake. Every game was competitive, which made for a better experience for all the kids.

It was the first day of school in a different state, and the kids had no friends. I guess you can say that this first day of school was not what we were used to. We nor the kids knew what to expect at this new school in Arlington Heights, Illinois. Well, it did not take long to find out that the fourth grade in Illinois was ahead of the same grade level in California. I tried to plead with them to just put Tim and Terry back a grade to the third grade, but they refused. Even though I explained in detail what the twins had gone through at birth and during the time their birth mother was pregnant with them. This was a difficult school year with Tim and Terry being diagnosed with ADHD and on medication, with a history of being developmentally delayed, but they still refused to drop a grade. The teachers would send all these notes home with all these demands that were just unrealistic.

The funny thing is that they advanced them to the fifth grade, which was ridiculous, in my opinion. Since the fourth grade was a disaster of a school year, I decided to do everything I could that summer to help the twins do better in the fifth grade. I guess it was Dad's summer school. I set out to make sure that the twins would learn their multiplication tables by heart and not only read books but also write essays on each book. I would read the book first, then have Tim and Terry read it to write an essay on that book. It was not a fun summer for them, but I couldn't let them go through that again. I was so proud of how well they did. Their attitudes were super good. At this point, I am falling increasingly in love with these two little guys.

As I go down memory lane to write this book, I realize just how special these twin boys were in my life. Tim and Terry made me a better man, without a doubt, in my opinion.

Towards the end of the year, Donte went back to San Diego, California, for good. He stayed with us for several years, but it was understood that he was a foster child only. We were not and couldn't adopt him because he was a verified Native American. Anyway, he went back, and it was going to happen eventually, regardless. Donte never wanted to travel with us to Illinois anyway, so it was inevitable. We spoke with him a few times after he left but slowly lost all communication with him.

CHAPTER 10

THE TENTH YEAR

The boys are now out of school for the summer, a great time to move again, but a local move after purchasing a home in South Elgin, Illinois. Even though we hired movers, I decided to have everything but furniture loaded in the garage to make it an easier operation for our movers. Everyone had their own bedroom, which brought excitement. This would mark the first time the twins did not have to share a bedroom together. South Elgin, Illinois, was a nice little village with nice neighbors up and down the street. Before we knew it, the kids had met new friends. For Tim and Terry, it was Vince and Charlie who, to this day, are all still friends. We bought a Trampoline for the kids years earlier and set it up. They played on this Trampoline a lot. I set up the basketball goal (yes, the same one from California), which almost became the neighborhood place to play basketball. Of course, I was the King of my driveway court as I took everyone to school every time someone showed up feeling lucky.

After the boys' baseball season, we took a road trip in our family van to where I grew up in Louisiana and got off to a great start. The kids got to see where I went to school, where I played little league baseball. Overall, it was a fun trip. Until it was time to leave Louisiana for Illinois. While leaving my hometown, we got rear-ended in Jennings, Louisiana, on an off-ramp of all places. It damaged the rear of the van and completely knocked out the rear window. Whitney was out of her seat belt for some reason and got injured during the accident. She hurt her neck, and we ended up in the emergency room at a nearby hospital. Thank goodness it ended up only being a minor injury, and we were able to continue our trip home. Well, after I rigged up a large cardboard to cover our missing rear window first.

The new puppy from the Humane Society (the pound) in Arlington Heights, Illinois, was an instant hit. We named him Lucky because we got him before they may have euthanized him. Luckily, the new puppy was so happy to have a new home. His little tail never stopped wagging. Lucky would become a family member and guard the kids very well, which I loved. Tim and

Terry produced this crazy game involving flatulence and burping where they would have to say "safety" if they had a gas incident. If another person said "doorknob" first, that person got to punch them until they grabbed a "doorknob." I witnessed this multiple times in our home.

The first baseball season in our new town of South Elgin ran into a bit of a problem. One day, the twins were coming to me complaining about not playing enough in their baseball games. So, I decided to teach Tim and Terry a life lesson when I got the chance to talk to their coach after one of their ball games. I approached Coach Mike with the boys by my side. I first explained to the coach that I was here on behalf of my two sons, Tim and Terry. They have brought to my attention that they are not getting enough playing time. I did one-eighty by turning their complaints back on them instead of on coach Mike. I told the coach that he was the authority on this field and team, just like their teacher was in his or her classrooms. I told the coach that whatever he decided for his team was his business. I told him that Tim and Terry would no longer be complaining about playing time. They will be working extra hard to "make themselves better" and will be taking responsibility for not being good enough to play more. At this point, Coach Mike was looking at me, speechless and in amazement. I never expected a speech like that from a parent.

I then turned to face my sons and told them this in front of their coach. "You need to do what other kids aren't willing to do today so that tomorrow, you will be doing things that they will be unable to do. It is not the coach's job to make you better. It is your job to do this." I also told the boys to never come to me with an excuse or complaint on why they are not playing more, impress your coach and earn the right to play more. Coach Mike shook my hand tightly and said he was impressed. Later that day, I explained to them why I did what I did. I told them simply that this was a lesson in responsibility, accountability, ethics and, more importantly, in this case, Teamwork. I said that when you are on the bench, it is your responsibility to stay focused on the game. By knowing the count of every batter, the score and the different situations going on in the game. In baseball, you never know when you might be needed in the game, so you must always be ready. Cheer your teammates on loudly, and be a great teammate. After each game, work on your game to get better. I let them know that I would help with that, and I did just that. In my opinion, to become a leader of men, you must first be a good follower. They never again complained about not playing enough to me ever again. To my knowledge, they may not have ever done it, even in their adult lives. When I say that I do not accept any excuses, I mean it. It was my way of teaching the boys that no one likes excuses, not your father, your future boss, a police officer...etc. An excuse means something didn't get done, or you are trying to exonerate yourself. So, with that being said, Tim and Terry knew that no excuse was ever accepted, but solutions were.

At seven years of age, it became apparent that Whitney was a legitimate artist. She would draw cartoon characters from watching television. Got her an appointment for private art instruction. This was a prominent artist with considerable experience. Well, after her first appointment, we were informed that Whitney's art skills were far more advanced than his skills.

I was blown away by this and realized at this point that we had a prodigy on our hands. This is all without ever going to any level of art school. Tim was also good at drawing, but even he said that Whitney was special. Incidentally, this causes Tim to sort of step to the side to allow his little sister the attention she needs. Tim, nonetheless, simply did a non-selfish act. I am so proud of him— On the first day of school, my twin boys were close to turning 10 years old.

They have come an exceptionally long way and continue to improve in every category of their development. They had a rough fourth grade, so I was apprehensive about the Fifth grade. They weren't nervous at all, so I just went along with their laid-back attitude. They were going with the right approach but were not really sure. First up was Tim's teacher, who needed to talk to his parents. It was a terrific opportunity to get a good rapport with his teacher. Well, Tim found out exactly how it would be between his father and his teacher. When his teacher explained the problem, I was totally on the teacher's side and let my son know it in front of his teacher. A funny thing happened after that; the problems Tim had with his teacher went away. I told the teacher to feel free to send extra homework home with Timothy. I told her that I would personally make sure it would get done. Later that year, Tim must have gotten amnesia because he came home complaining about how his teacher was doing something in class. I stayed perfectly quiet as I listened to everything he had to say. After he was done, I made two points. The first question I asked was, which classroom is it? Tim said it was the teacher's classroom (good answer). The second question was, who has the college degree and has obtained their teaching credentials, you, Tim, or your teacher? At this point, Tim was getting upset because he knew this was a losing battle on his part. So, to end the whole thing, I offered to go in and talk with his teacher on the matter.

He said no quickly because he remembered what happened the last time I talked to his teacher. He got the opposite of what he wanted: extra homework and a father who sided with his teacher. Do you know that that was the very last time either twin boy ever had a problem with a teacher again? Mission accomplished with a very good understanding of my rule of not looking for excuses in life.

Patrick visits for the first time and almost gets attacked by our dog Lucky, who was protecting Whitney. Patrick arrives, and we talk with each other in the driveway, with Tim and Terry listening. Patrick needed to use the restroom, and I totally forgot about Whitney being inside along with Lucky. He enters our home, and after a moment or so, we hear Patrick yell out, "Your dog"! We ran into the house and rescued him just in the nick of time from our dog Lucky.

I started cutting grass at age nine years old, so why not have Tim and Terry learn how to cut the grass? I began training them in the art of cutting grass. Now, nothing I do is easy, meaning not only did they learn how to cut grass, but they also had to learn Lawnmower maintenance and clean up afterward. I took the boys over to our next-door neighbor's house to ask her if she needed her grass cut. She said yes, and I assured her that I would be supervising them. In no time at all, they became good at it, and I finally turned them loose. The deal was that each boy had to cut the lady's yard together, and each would make five dollars. Their total amount received was eleven dollars, with one dollar paid to their father (me) for Lawn Mower rental, fuel and oil. I wanted the twins to get comfortable working and earning money. All other money they received to this point was what I called "free money" money given to them, not earned. My sons were now entrepreneurs, just as I once was at nine years old. I was so proud of them during this period of their life. So many people had given them almost no chance of being productive citizens, but it was my mission to prove everyone wrong. At this point in Tim and Terry's lives, they have proved the naysayers wrong.

The White Sox home game is a first for both boys, including myself. They were so excited, which made me happy. We went to the game and spent too much money, but it was my boys' first trip to a Major League Baseball game in Chicago. I think I took them to a San Diego Padres game once, but they were so young I don't think they would remember it like this game. The twins got to go and run the bases after the baseball game. I was so touched by their pure joy as they walked back up to me and gave me a big hug on our way home. One of the biggest thunderstorms I have ever experienced in my life happened while we were heading home on the I-290 freeway. Terry freaked out and thought it was the end of the world from the way he was reacting. The storm was over in no time, and we continued home.

Baseball time again, and Tim and Terry were ready to go at it. One of my favorite things that I loved doing with them was purchasing their baseball gear. I got them a new bat and bag, and then we had batting practice almost every day. In fact, every year, I got them a new bat, batting bag and other related baseball gear. I also got them new baseball cleats and a new baseball glove, which was necessary. The older they got, the more things they needed or wanted. Remember the need vs want thing in the future. Terry ended up having a tremendous season as his brother struggled but was supportive of Terry and his successes. Terry was invited to join the all-star team with a chance to go to the Little League World Series. They didn't make it, but Terry had a great game, and I enjoyed every minute of his final game.

The coach allowed Tim to be on the team even though he did not make the All-Star Team because he did not want to separate the twins. Tim was a good sport by cheering his brother on. I was so proud of him for being there for Terry.

Got the boy's hockey sticks and a street puck, and bam! There we were, playing street hockey competitively against each other. That was so much fun. I can still remember that time as clear as day. One day, the kids were outside playing when I heard Whitney come in crying. She was complaining about her finger hurting. I must have forgotten that I was talking to a little girl and instead to one of the boys. So, I said, Oh Ah, it's alright, just wait for it to stop hurting and then start playing again. She wasn't having it and insisted something was wrong. Well, later at the emergency room, it turned out to be not only a fracture on the finger and hand, according to the doctor, but they also needed to put a hard cast on it. I felt bad for not being more concerned when she first came to me.

It's a beautiful Autumn Day in the suburbs of Chicago, and it's that time of the year for raking up leaves and then bagging them for disposal. It's time for me to go to work, but there are a ton of leaves in the backyard. So, I called Tim and Terry out to help take care of the leaves. I helped them rake all the leaves into piles to be bagged. I showed them how to bag a few bags of leaves and watched them bag a bag of leaves by themselves. Now comes the command. I told them that I wanted all the leaves placed in bags and then transferred them to the curb for pick up. Snow was coming later that week, and I didn't want to deal with wet, frozen leaves. I explained all of this to them. Finally, I told them if the leaves were not picked up completely by the time I got home at four in the morning, I would get them both out of bed. Then they would finish in the cold and dark while I would watch them while drinking my coffee. Got home at four in the morning, as I said I would, and nothing had been done. I woke them up, and sure enough, I sat there drinking coffee as they bagged all the leaves. From that day forward, I was never disobeyed like that again.

CHAPTER 11

THE ELEVENTH YEAR

The basement bathroom construction was an all-hands effort, meaning the kids and I. We would be removing and replacing the Toilet and painting a brick wall. It was an incredibly special time for me because I just loved doing things with all three kids. When it came time to install the toilet tank parts, I asked Terry to help with that.

Now, before I continue with this story, I must first explain how Tim was mechanically inclined and loved getting his hands dirty. Whitney was helpful, but I kept her on easy tasks, and that's just the way I operated with her. Terry, on the other hand, was not mechanically inclined at all. He hated manual labor of any kind. That will all change once he buys a car in the future and finds out who will be working on it (him)!

Here we go. I told Terry to remove the cover from the tank, and I got involved with another task with one of the other kids. When I turn around, I see Terry removing the entire tank. I yelled out. All I wanted was the cover removed from the tank. I showed him how to remove the cover, and without hesitation, Terry said out loud, "I'm an idiot." We were all on the floor in full-fledged, non-stop laughter with tears. Terry tried to hold back but finally broke into laughter along with his siblings and me. This one incident will never be forgotten for as long as we all shall live.

Tim came home one day saying that he let some kid wear his Izod shirt. When he tried to get it back from the kid, the kid refused to give it back to him. It was a gift; I believe it was an expensive shirt. So, it became a situation in our household. Well, it came down to contacting the kid's parents and getting the shirt back. A lesson learned by our children: to never lend out their clothes to children without permission.

One day, the kid's maternal grandma comes over with a skateboard for Terry. Twins or not, young kids can not be left out on gifts' no matter what the reason. I straight up questioned her about what she got for Tim. Whitney couldn't care less, especially since we spoiled her all the time. Tim was visibly hurt, so I took him out immediately and bought him a skateboard. Now, keeping their Grandma Marlene on the subject, another incident arose involving her inadvertently. I was putting a toy on time-out because the boys were fighting over it. Unexpectedly, Terry explained to me that his grandma bought it for him. My words to him and his brother were, "In my office, ASAP!" Once there, I explained to both boys that anything that enters this house, I own it. I told them that I didn't care if Peter Pan gave them something; I still needed to know about it. If I don't know about it, I will donate it to a child in need. I explained to them that I was like a Dictator or even a King. I also told them that they didn't understand it then but that one day they would and that it was for their own good.

While at a University of Notre Dame football game with my friend Patrick, I got a call that my Aunt Dean had passed away. She was my favorite Aunt and connected to my life in an unorthodox way. It was a love triangle involving my mother and my Aunt Dean's husband (my uncle/father). I will explain all of this later in the Author's Notes. There was absolutely no way I was going to miss her funeral. I took Tim and Terry to a department store and bought them suits and then drove to O'hare International Airport in Chicago to rent a car for our trip to Houston, Texas. I drove straight to Houston non-stop and attended the funeral. After visiting with all my relatives, I loaded up the twins, and I drove non-stop back to Chicago.

Yes, I never slept because I did not want the twins to miss any school. When it comes to my children's education, I will go the extra mile to make sure that they do not miss any school. They had perfect attendance, and I was not messing that up. RIP, Aunt Dean, with much love until we meet again; I love you to the moon and back.

One of the boys did something with my tools, which, for safety reasons, was forbidden without supervision by an adult. When I went in there to interrupt their video game, the mood was not good. I asked, who messed with my tools? Terry said it was not him (he was telling the truth), and Tim said it was not him (a lie). I drilled them until the truth came out. Then, I made a move that was different from what they expected. Terry was already preparing to resume his video game, and Tim was expecting punishment. I informed them that they would both be punished because I expect total honesty when I ask a direct question like that. I told them that Tim should have spoken right up and admitted his iniquity against me and his brother.

I told him that he knew it was wrong what he did. Therefore, it was his job to tell me, his father, that he played around with my tools. Before, I had to ask about the infraction, or at least answer once I asked, to admit it. I told Tim and Terry that if you keep a secret away like that or hide it, it is the same as lying. I told Tim what his punishment was, and he did it without any indignation. When I told Terry his punishment, he was mad but kept it under control. I explained to Terry later, after he was over his anger, that my question to them was, "Who was messing with my tools"? I told him that he should have said nothing if he was innocent. Sometimes, it is good for the innocent to remain silent unless directly addressed. I explained later to them that it was a reproach against me. Even though they were the ones punished, it was I who was the injured one. I know this all seems like a lot for ten-year-old boys, but I say no. It is all a process to transform these boys into "Alpha Males" when they become adults.

The trip to San Diego, California, was a blast for all of us. We even rented a Limo service to and from the airport. The kids were so excited to ride in a Limo for the first time. Rented a car once we landed in San Diego, and off, we went. We stayed at Kelli's sisters' home and enjoyed an exciting vacation. This one trip really went a long way in our family's cohesiveness. It was a positive trip from start to finish.

Baseball season number two at South Elgin's Little League. The previous year, Terry had a great season and was named to the all-star team (with a chance to go to the Little League World Series). Yes, it was an exciting time for our household as the twins excelled in baseball. They wound up not making it, but we were still excited about this season. I went out and bought a bunch of baseball gear. Some needed, and some we did not but just wanted. They went undefeated, and this time, it was Tim who was good, while Terry wasn't as good as he was the prior year. Perhaps he was injured and just played through it. That is what I would have done, and I just pushed through it with no excuses. Tim makes it to the All-Stars, and as of the prior year, Terry was allowed to accompany his brother since they were twins. During the All-Star baseball tournament, Tim's team was in an elimination game and lost. The problem here is that Tim was the last out of a miscommunication situation. Tim was the potential tying run at third base. The Pitcher throws a wild pitch, and it gets past the catcher. There was so much noise coming from the stands and dugout (third base dugout). Some yell out for Tim to go, and some, along with his coach, yell the opposite (to stay). Tim got confused, and he was then called out by the umpire on a bang-bang play at home plate. This is when the runner gets tagged by the person who caught the ball within seconds, whether the runner was about to make it to the base or while they were running. Afterward, people were yelling at Tim as if he made a mistake. I held onto the field to protect my son from my left field location. I knew whose fault it was immediately. It was the head coach, meaning he should have sensed the gravity of the situation. All the confusing noises and simply should have called a "TIME OUT!" Doing so would have taken control back and come up with a signal or something from the third base coach. Tim wanted to quit baseball after this and cried all the way home. We sat on the garage steps alone as he cried in my arms. I just comforted him and kept my comments to myself. As time passed, I finally explained to him that it was not his fault. It was a bang-bang play that happens in baseball all the time. I told him that this is how sports was. You can be a hero or not in an instant. I thought that he was safe, but in all honesty, I was way too far away. I thought this was a very good growing-up moment for him and for all of us since we all experienced it together.

It is the first day of school, and the twins are almost eleven years old as they enter the sixth grade. There is an annual sixth-grade trip that was always to Lake Geneva, Wisconsin, a famous Sky resort, boating, and fishing vacation place. It was marked as the first time Tim and Terry would be away from home by themselves. I was naturally a little nervous, but they were with their friend Vince. Knowing Terry, he had many more friends like Anthony on the trip. All went well with no problems and was a complete success.

Giant change to our whole family dynamic by way of my extended family in Louisiana. My mother would be coming to live with us. My sister Paula and her two girls, Latroya and Sobridy, all ended up tagging along with my mother, Melba. My sister convinced me that she would only be with us temporarily.

Since she would be transferring from her Pharmacy job in Louisiana to the same company in the area where we lived. Tension was built while they stayed with us. My children did not do well with this setup and made it known to me on more than one occasion. Mainly, Tim was saying to me that he likes it better when it's just us. I was forced to get my sister to move

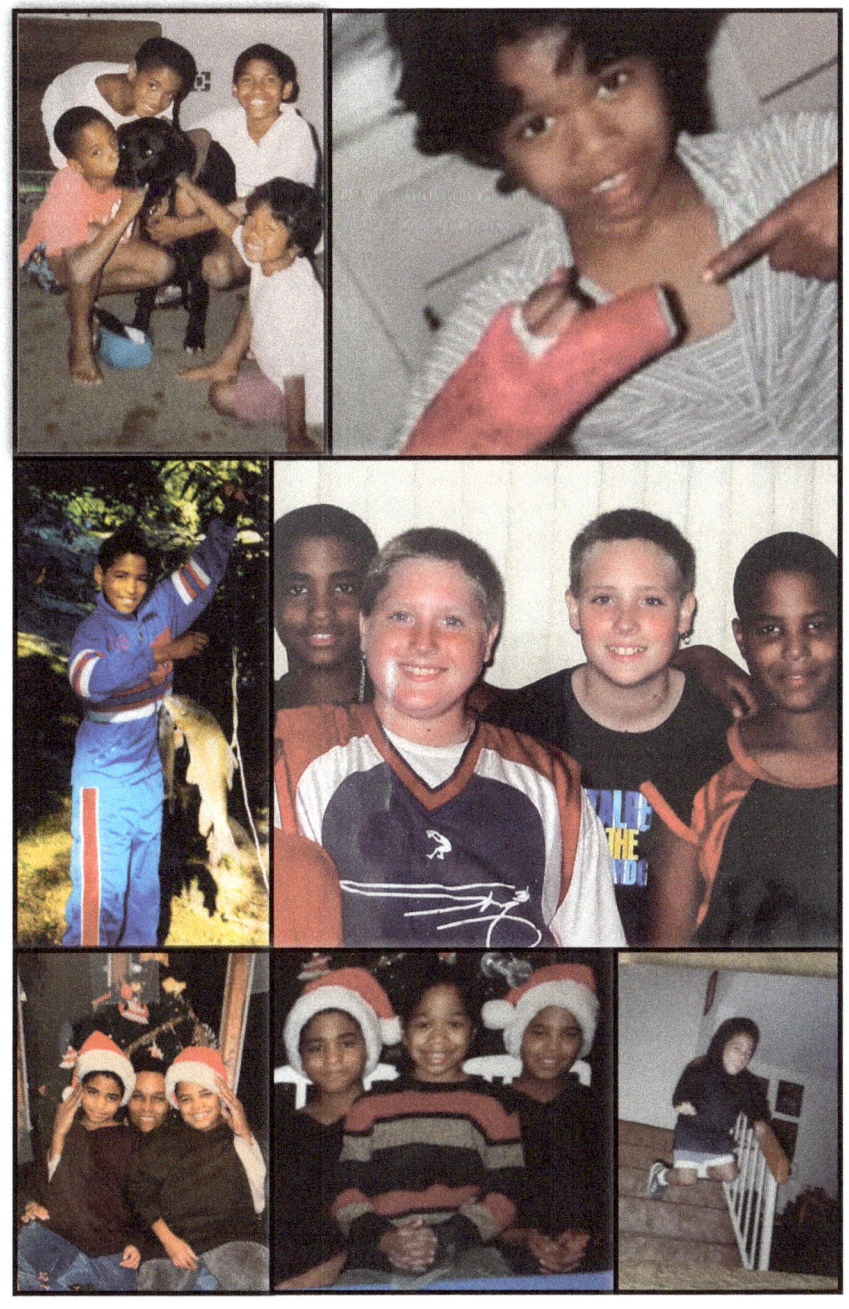

out by a certain date just to make sure there were no misunderstandings. Paula and her two daughters moved out, and my mother stayed with us as originally planned (Tim was okay with that). The tension I had seen developing in my kids seemed to disappear instantly once they moved out. I Promised I would never do that again to my children.

CHAPTER 12

THE TWELFTH YEAR

Unwritten rules are established because it was time. Remember that most of this does not apply to Whitney because I was raising her differently than her twin brothers on purpose. A trend started up with Tim and Terry about material things. They were confusing need with want, and it was up to me to rectify this discrepancy before it got out of hand. A perfect example of this was when shopping for school clothes. They wanted expensive items like name-brand jeans and sneakers. Another example would be if their teacher wanted a certain expensive item for a class that could be substituted with a household item, I would send them with the household item. I did this to show the boy's items can be substituted. I started getting a lot of this from the boys, "everyone is doing this or buying that." I got tired of telling the boys the old, caged answer I always got when I was begging for things when I was a kid, "If everyone jumped off the roof on their heads, would you want to do as they did"? I developed the want or need test on everything they wanted. With a disclaimer attached that not all things you need will be possible to get sometimes. When I would get the old, I want this that everyone else is getting, I would ask them if it was a needed or wanted item. This ended a lot of frustrating and never-ending begging. Dad's Psychology 101 worked to perfection.

Another saying I would tell the boys often (in the third person) was, "Your father is never wrong. He is always right." This way, we will never have to argue about anything since your father is always right. They would complain about it, and I would just give them the same old tired example. For instance, "if your father says that the sky is green, and you look at it and see it's obviously blue," It's green, end of the story.

The Next thing was excuses not being accepted by me. I accepted no excuses, and that went for things even if they were obvious. I was firm on this one because to become an Alpha Male, you cannot use excuses, in my opinion. I taught the twins that you must improvise, adapt, and overcome, and none of these is possible if you use excuses. I told them that you cannot have integrity and be responsible by using excuses. Be honest and look the person in the eye as you shake their hand firmly. Also, look a person in the eyes when communicating with them. Learn to know when you are being disrespected by the lack of eye-to-eye contact with others while communicating. So yes, if you make eye contact, you are being respected. The bottom line is this: I accepted no excuses from Tim and Terry, and because of that, I honestly believe they got closer to becoming honorable men each time they had an opportunity to give an excuse but did not.

A few other rules my twin boys had to adhere to was once the sun went down, they had to be in the house. Another was an older one, but important enough to re-visit. It was anything that came into our home. I had to know about it. Once, I had a Police officer knock on my door. He wanted to talk to Tim and Terry about an accusation, accusing them of firing paint guns at houses. A Kid from the neighborhood turned Tim and Terry's names into the police. When I had the officer wait while I went to get the boys, I told them to only talk if I said to talk. I said nothing and let the Police officer get it all out. Tim and Terry never opened their mouths, so I did all the talking except for one question when I asked the boys if they had paint guns in my house without my knowledge. They said no and went back to being silent. I told the Police officer that I do not know where you got this information from, but Tim and Terry are never out of this house after sundown. The incident supposedly occurred at ten o'clock at night. I explained to the officer that there was no way possible for my boys to be out since bedtime is at nine o'clock every weeknight. I told the officer that I had surveillance cameras set up in the common areas to make sure there were not any shenanigans going on after bedtime. I made sure that the officer understood that these boys were my responsibility, and I was determined to raise them to be law-abiding and productive citizens. The Police officer was very impressed and left my home, certain my two boys were not involved in any way with the paintballing of houses in our neighborhood. We never heard about it again, so all was okay. Both rules proved their effectiveness in this incident. Nothing comes into the house without their father's knowledge and to have yourselves in the house before dark.

We bought an old Van for my mother to drive and a tent camper on wheels. We put both into effective use on a family camping trip to Indiana. The place was called Indiana Beach Campgrounds in Monticello, Indiana. I remember it being a fun time of relaxation and playing around with the kids a lot. There was a lot to do here, including a Go Kart Racing Park. Terry was the champion as he bumped me out of the way, and even I could not complain since excuses are not accepted in our little world (practice what you preach, Marvin). We loved the tent camper and were satisfied with the Dodge Caravan Van with a Mitsubishi engine in it instead of a Dodge engine (odd).

The twins played baseball on a team and on their own all summer long. They rode their bikes all over the neighborhood, enjoying newfound freedom. I trusted them. Lying was not even in our vocabulary. The boys went fishing all the time as well. They kept busy outside on the go, which I liked. It reminded me of my own childhood when I was their

age. One thing that really made me proud was when, one day, I took the twins to a Chinese restaurant. Tim and Terry were eleven years old, and at ten years old, they would have been considered for the child rate. When we got to the cashier, the lady asked me what age Tim and Terry were. I hesitated for a moment, and Tim spoke up with the truth, their real age. I have never been prouder. To say the least, the boys truly enjoyed the summer of 2002 as they neared twelve years old.

This was also the summer we would start filling our home up with many pets (the wild kingdom). It felt like the wild kingdom of Omaha as pets started joining our family. Okay, first, there were two new dogs besides Lucky. These new dogs were Milo and Daisy. Then came three cats, all at separate times. One cat was named Romeo for Terry, and for Tim, it was Fefe; the name of Whitney's cat was Puff Daddy. We got a Rat for Tim named Patches. Terry got the Hamster, which later got out of his cage and was eaten by one of the other animals. My money was on Lucky because it may have bitten Lucky and paid the ultimate price.

It was the first day of the seventh grade, as the twins were nearly twelve years old. They have been re-zoned and must spend two years in an Elgin middle school for seventh and eighth grades. Then, it would be off to Elgin High School for the ninth grade before finally going to the brand-new South Elgin High School. They ended up being the first students at the new South Elgin High School with only a tenth and eleventh grade.

Basketball battles were legendary in our driveway. My daughter, who was just eight years old, was very good at sports, especially basketball and softball. She would play with us sometimes and hold her own. Of course, if anyone got too rough with her, I would simply not allow that person to score again.

I was the King of the court (Bar Nun), and everyone knew it. Tim and Terry tried so hard to beat me, and I never made it easy on them. They knew that coming in because I told them if they beat me, everyone else would be easier. The only thing stopping some of those games was darkness, and of course, darkness meant in the house, no questions asked. I would spend time with them with pleasure because I loved being around my kids. The kids and I would also ride our bikes on long trips together. Whitney was tough enough to hang with her brothers fairly well. I would go fishing with the boys a lot, but they would run me down by the end of the weekend. I would rest during my work week, which included weightlifting after work. I wanted to set an example for all three of my kids by keeping a stiff regimen of weightlifting so they could hopefully follow my example by being physically fit.

Unwritten rules are established because it was time. Remember that most of this does not apply to Whitney because I was raising her differently than her twin brothers on purpose. A trend started up with Tim and Terry about material things. They were confusing need with want, and it was up to me to rectify this discrepancy before it got out of hand. A perfect example of this was when shopping for school clothes. They wanted expensive items like name-brand jeans and sneakers. Another example would be if their teacher wanted a certain expensive item for a class that could be substituted with a household item, I would send them with the household item. I did this to show the boy's items can be substituted. I started getting a lot of this from the boys, "everyone is doing this or buying that." I got tired of telling the boys the old, caged answer I always got when I was begging for things when I was a kid, "If everyone jumped off the roof on their heads, would you want to do as they did"? I developed the want or need test on everything they wanted. With a disclaimer attached that not all things you need will be possible to get sometimes. When I would get the old, I want this that everyone else is getting, I would ask them if it was a needed or wanted item. This ended a lot of frustrating and never-ending begging. Dad's Psychology 101 worked to perfection.

Another saying I would tell the boys often (in the third person) was, "Your father is never wrong. He is always right." This way, we will never have to argue about anything since your father is always right. They would complain about it, and I would just give them the same old tired example. For instance, "if your father says that the sky is green, and you look at it and see it's obviously blue," It's green, end of the story.

The Next thing was excuses not being accepted by me. I accepted no excuses, and that went for things even if they were obvious. I was firm on this one because to become an Alpha Male, you cannot use excuses, in my opinion. I taught the twins that you must improvise, adapt, and overcome, and none of these is possible if you use excuses. I told them that you cannot have integrity and be responsible by using excuses. Be honest and look the person in the eye as you shake their hand firmly. Also, look a person in the eyes when communicating with them. Learn to know when you are being disrespected by the lack of eye-to-eye contact with others while communicating. So yes, if you make eye contact, you are being respected. The bottom line is this: I accepted no excuses from Tim and Terry, and because of that, I honestly believe they got closer to becoming honorable men each time they had an opportunity to give an excuse but did not.

A few other rules my twin boys had to adhere to was once the sun went down, they had to be in the house. Another was an older one, but important enough to re-visit. It was anything that came into our home. I had to know about it. Once, I had a Police officer knock on my door. He wanted to talk to Tim and Terry about an accusation, accusing them of firing paint guns at houses. A Kid from the neighborhood turned Tim and Terry's names into the police. When I had the officer wait while I went to get the boys, I told them to only talk if I said to talk. I said nothing and let the Police officer get it all out. Tim and Terry never opened their mouths, so I did all the talking except for one question when I asked the boys if they had paint guns in my house without my knowledge. They said no and went back to being silent. I told the Police officer that I do not know where you got this information from, but Tim and Terry are never out of this house after sundown. The incident supposedly occurred at ten o'clock at night. I explained to the officer that there was no way possible for my boys to be out since bedtime is at nine o'clock every weeknight. I told the officer that I had surveillance cameras set up in the common areas to make sure there were not any shenanigans going on after bedtime. I made sure that the officer understood that these boys were my responsibility, and I was determined to raise them to be law-abiding and productive citizens. The Police officer was very impressed and left my home, certain my two boys were not involved in any way with the paintballing of houses in our neighborhood. We never heard about it again, so all was okay. Both rules proved their effectiveness in this incident. Nothing comes into the house without their father's knowledge and to have yourselves in the house before dark.

We bought an old Van for my mother to drive and a tent camper on wheels. We put both into effective use on a family camping trip to Indiana. The place was called Indiana Beach Campgrounds in Monticello, Indiana. I remember it being a fun time of relaxation and playing around with the kids a lot. There was a lot to do here, including a Go Kart Racing Park. Terry was the champion as he bumped me out of the way, and even I could not complain since excuses are not accepted in our little world (practice what you preach, Marvin). We loved the tent camper and were satisfied with the Dodge Caravan Van with a Mitsubishi engine in it instead of a Dodge engine (odd).

The twins played baseball on a team and on their own all summer long. They rode their bikes all over the neighborhood, enjoying newfound freedom. I trusted them. Lying was not even in our vocabulary. The boys went fishing all the time as well. They kept busy outside on the go, which I liked. It reminded me of my own childhood when I was their age. One thing that really made me proud was when, one day, I took the twins to a Chinese restaurant. Tim and Terry were eleven years old, and at ten years old, they would have been considered for the child rate. When we got to the cashier, the lady asked me what age Tim and Terry were. I hesitated for a moment, and Tim spoke up with the truth, their real age. I have never been prouder. To say the least, the boys truly enjoyed the summer of 2002 as they neared twelve years old.

This was also the summer we would start filling our home up with many pets (the wild kingdom). It felt like the wild kingdom of Omaha as pets started joining our family. Okay, first, there were two new dogs besides Lucky. These new dogs were Milo and Daisy. Then came three cats, all at separate times. One cat was named Romeo for Terry, and for Tim, it was Fefe; the name of Whitney's cat was Puff Daddy. We got a Rat for Tim named Patches. Terry got the Hamster, which later got out of his cage and

66

was eaten by one of the other animals. My money was on Lucky because it may have bitten Lucky and paid the ultimate price.

It was the first day of the seventh grade, as the twins were nearly twelve years old. They have been re-zoned and must spend two years in an Elgin middle school for seventh and eighth grades. Then, it would be off to Elgin High School for the ninth grade before finally going to the brand-new South Elgin High School. They ended up being the first students at the new South Elgin High School with only a tenth and eleventh grade.

Basketball battles were legendary in our driveway. My daughter, who was just eight years old, was very good at sports, especially basketball and softball. She would play with us sometimes and hold her own. Of course, if anyone got too rough with her, I would simply not allow that person to score again.

I was the King of the court (Bar Nun), and everyone knew it. Tim and Terry tried so hard to beat me, and I never made it easy on them. They knew that coming in because I told them if they beat me, everyone else would be easier. The only thing stopping some of those games was darkness, and of course, darkness meant in the house, no questions asked. I would spend time with them with pleasure because I loved being around my kids. The kids and I would also ride our bikes on long trips together. Whitney was tough enough to hang with her brothers fairly well. I would go fishing with the boys a lot, but they would run me down by the end of the weekend. I would rest during my work week, which included weightlifting after work. I wanted to set an example for all three of my kids by keeping a stiff regimen of weightlifting so they could hopefully follow my example by being physically fit.

CHAPTER 13

THE THIRTEENTH YEAR

One day, Whiney and her best friend Alexandria (Alex) were out selling raffle tickets to raise money for their girls' softball team. Alex's dad, Chip and I both gave them instructions on what to do and what not to do while selling tickets. They had a limited area in which they were authorized to sell tickets, and all seemed okay. Well, it was brought to my attention that both girls went into a man's home to wait for the money for tickets. A complete violation of our rules. Picture two nine-year-old girls dressed in their softball jerseys and as vulnerable as could be. This incident led to operation sexual offenders, child trafficking and bad people who seem nice but are not and will do horrible things to boys and girls. I went in depth with my kids about how children are taken by these bad people and killed after they do terrible things to them. Many times, these bad people will be someone that you know. My kids first asked me why and what terrible things. I went from child to child, asking them what the answers were to those questions. They surprisingly produced some great answers, like rape and that they kill so that the child will not be able to tell on them to their parents or the police. We went into just what Raping and Molesting a child meant. I was prepared with information that I downloaded off our computer. Even though the kids were missing out on playing time, they were not complaining. The next step was going over the information on printed paper I had taped over an entire wall. It was a list of all the sexual predators in South Elgin. I went from house to house to point out all the houses highlighted in yellow. Those were the registered sex offenders by street name and personal addresses. After going over all of this for about an hour and a half, I did something dramatic so that the kids would always remember this training. I walked up to the wall where all the information was taped to the wall and ripped it all down, balled it up and threw it all in the trash can.

The look on my three kids' faces was a look of total disbelief and fear. It had a dramatic effect, but most importantly, it got their attention. They asked a few nervous questions, which I answered promptly. I told them that I ripped down everything because no one could know just how many sexual predators are out there. Some may have never been caught yet. So, you are forbidden from trusting anyone. You need permission from either me or your mom to go into anyone's home or car. It must be our voice and not someone telling you we told them to tell you it was all right. This means that if someone other than you or your mom is picking you up in a car, you are not to get in that car, no matter what they say. You must hear it come out of your mom or dad's mouth only, even if you know the person, like a relative, neighbor, family friend or anyone else. Remember, they may tell you that your mom or dad is in the hospital and told me to pick you up, NO! Do not get in that car unless you hear it come from your parents' mouth. Never allow yourself to be placed in someone's car, no matter what they tell you. If they say, they will kill you if you don't, run away from them and make lots of noise. If they grab you, fight and make as much noise as you can make. If they get you in the car, you will never be seen alive again. From this day forward, you are not to talk to any strangers for any reason when you are alone. If you suspect anything not being right (a gut feeling), tell your teacher, a police officer, the principal and always your parents. Bad people will try and scare you by saying things like, if you do not, I will kill your mom and dad. Don't believe them. Fight and be loud. Your body is forbidden from anyone touching you inappropriately by any person, including your mom and dad. If anyone ever touches you, tell the first adult if you are not around your parents. That bad person will try to tell you not to tell on them, tell them OK and that you will not tell, but tell anyway. As soon as you are safely away from the person, tell everything that happened to a trusted adult or authority. Remember this for as long as you shall live (I told them).

Always remember this point: if something is not wrong, there will be no need for secrecy. On the other hand, if something is wrong, you will know it because the person will be doing it in secrecy. An example would be if you wanted to ride your bike on a busy street like Randle Road, which is an extremely dangerous road. If you asked me if you could ride your bike on this road, what do you think my answer would be every time? No, right? Well, if you do not ask and do it anyway, will you tell me that you did this dangerous thing? Probably not, because you know it is wrong, and you had to do it in secrecy. Just like the bad person who knows it is a terrible thing that they are doing to you, and yet they don't want anyone to know. Tell me everything because I can save you from harm. Now you kids know why I am so overprotective.

The first day of school for eighth grade was a predictable first day where the kids were all in good moods. I had taken the boys to get new school clothes and somehow did an okay job at it. I cannot be confused for anyone with a taste for fashion, believe me. Taking them back to school shopping would end up being a trend for the three of us in getting their new school clothes and shoes. The twins would be turning thirteen years old soon, and the signs of puberty had already begun. They had stopped wanting to be dressed the same anymore a year earlier. Now, it had to be unmistakably different. There was starting to be some drama at these school clothes-shopping events. At the end of the day, I had the final say if it got to that point, which they did everything in their power to avoid (I do not blame them since I am terrible at fashion). For the most part, Tim and Terry wanted no part of Dad intervening at all. As I said, puberty was in the beginning stages and happening fast. We got the squeaky voices and very confused young teens trying to deal with all the changes to their bodies. I believe girls process these changes much better than knucklehead boys, especially when it comes to asking questions like why is this happening to me?

There was an incident on the bus where a neighbor kid, Jammie (who I called Harry Potter because he looked just like him). Anyway, Harry Potter decided to pick on Terry while they were riding home from school on the bus. Tim stood up for his brother as he often did, and I guess Harry Potter did not like that. I happened to be home when they returned home from the bus. As I awaited both boys to come home, there was something not right as they entered our driveway. Terry was crying while Tim was in an argument with Harry Potter. I just watched from our front window. Next thing I know, Tim comes running out of our garage with a hockey stick and swinging it with the intention to harm Harry Potter. Now, Tim and Terry were in Middle School (eighth grade) while Harry Potter (Jammie) was in High School and a lot older than Tim and Terry. By the time I made it outside, Harry Potter was on his way home. That kid never messed with Terry again and understood that Tim was not trying to scare him. He was trying to do great bodily harm to him.

Up to this point, the boys had only played baseball as it pertains to sports. So, we decided to put Tim, Terry, and Whitney into Karate. It was good for them to have to learn discipline as they would show this moving up in belt ranks. Looked like dancing to me. They all three made it from white belt to yellow belt. It was a big step, or so I was told. I was proud of them as they had to demonstrate that they could, in fact, complete the moves required to advance to the yellow belt.

Next up was basketball, where I could coach Terry. Tim landed on one of the other teams. That was as rewarding to me as it was for the boys. I have to say that both Tim and Terry did a fantastic job operating in the team sport concept. There were a couple of times that I had to intervene when my boys and teammates would attempt to blame others for losses. I explained to them all that there was no 'I' in team. Moreover, in a soft approach, I said that when you are on a team, you are one. If a teammate makes a mistake, it is incumbent upon every teammate to make up for that mistake. I told them to never give excuses but instead be responsible by putting their teammates first ahead of themselves. If every teammate does this, you will be a true team. Again, when you make a mistake in the game, I expect all your teammates to pick you up. I expect them all, playing or not, to rally around you and make it their business to make up for whatever mistake was made. In baseball, for instance, a ball is not caught in the outfield by the left fielder. A run scored that would not have been scored because it would have been the third out. It is the duty of the rest of the team to pick him or her up and not ridicule him or her. The team needs to go out and get that run back, and if they don't, the team loses as a team. The point is this: The left fielder didn't lose the game.

Tim and Terry decided to try out for Football for their middle school team of sixth, seventh and eighth graders. At the time, they were having some problems with their grades. We were asked to a meeting with their teachers, the school Counselor and the Principal. Kelli and I explained the situation for both boys up to this point in their schooling. We explained that they needed extra help beyond normal classroom help. For instance, pulling out of class for more one-on-one instruction. Another way of teaching them differently in class that they struggled in. I got irritated with this meeting because they were not following us on exactly what the twins had come from (birth to now). Just how much of a leap forward they had accomplished. I finally told them to hold them back a year, especially since they were below their class age by one year. The reason for this is that in California, where they began attending school, they started a year earlier than in Illinois. Every one of their classmates was a full year older than Tim and Terry. Incidentally, the twins were developmentally delayed. Nonetheless, when I returned home, the boys beat me to the punch. Telling me that they had quit the football team. Just when I was prepared to inform them that I was taking them off the team due to bad grades. Earlier that day at football practice, Terry got hit hard. A term we used in football when I played was, "He got the snot knocked out of him." It was his former teammate, Hakeem, from their little league team. A noticeably big young man who was strong. That was that, but there were still issues that I had to address with both Tim and Terry. I asked them if they realized how bad their grades were, and I got eyes to the floor while they mumbled. I informed them that I was going to take them off the football team anyway, but there was no reaction. I told them no TV or video games for the entire semester until their grades improved. Then, I physically unhooked everything and hauled it all up to my bedroom. It was the video game machine, the TV itself and the VCR, mainly for effect. After all that commotion, you would never believe that a humorous moment would happen. It was Tim, who said with a straight face as if he were some comedian, "All you had to take was the TV." Of course, he was 100% right, and I had to bite my bottom lip not to laugh. Get it; everything's hooked up to the TV! That whole time period until their grades improved was like a soap opera, mostly with Terry. Tim hit the books hard and improved his grades. He did not seem as disturbed by the punishment as Terry was. Terry would rush through his homework to finish first and then would come upstairs to make a big mistake. He would say I did not have anything to do and that he was bored. I started giving him stuff to do, and that solved that problem in a hurry.

I'm ex-military with all types of ideals to ruin a day quickly. Suddenly, Terry had plenty to do, "HOMEWORK"! When report card time was ready, they brought up their grades significantly. From this time forward, Tim and Terry were able to make reasonably good grades. They got caught up (just like I did) in the long-standing "developmentally delayed term that they had heard forever." Turns out, Tim and Terry were just being lazy.

One day, Whitney and her friend Alex came home after school and told me that Jammie, a.k.a. Harry Potter, was messing with them at their bus stop in the morning. This was two fifth graders being disturbed by a high school student. First Terry and now my daughter and her friend. I made some calls and found out that it is a violation to be at the wrong bus stop with younger children. I was planning to go down to their bus stop to nip this thing in the bud. As we discussed this, Tim and Terry said that they would handle this with their friends Vince and Charlie. I said OK, make sure he understands that it is inappropriate for him to be at the girl's bus stop. The very next day, the four boys walked Whitney and her friend Alex to their bus stop. About half an hour later, the four boys stop by the house on their way to their bus stop. They informed me that they got into a fight with Harry Potter and broke his eyeglasses. Basically, they beat up a high school student. That evening, I got a knock on my door. I answered the door to find Harry Potter and his angry mother standing there. I say, is there something I could help them with? Harry Potter's mom tells me that Tim and Terry broke their son's eyeglasses. I told her to wait for a minute while I got my son's "front and center"! When the boys arrived upstairs, I asked them, did you break Jammie's (Harry Potter) eyeglasses and they said in unison, yes, we did. I let them explain. They said that Jammie was harassing Whitney and Alex. I told Jammie's mom that her son was not supposed to be at that bus stop with the younger children. I said that he could get in trouble for that if I decided to report it. His mom looked dumbfounded, while Tim and Terry were as melancholy as could be. I told her that Vince and Charlie were also there to do what I asked them to do: walk the girls to their bus stop because they complained about Jammie harassing them. Her face turned red, and obviously, her son left out a lot of his side of the story. Finally, getting annoyed, I asked this lady if there was anything else I could help her with, and she said no! I looked right into Harry Potter's eyes and told him that I did not appreciate him at my daughter's bus stop. I told him that if he continued harassing my daughter and her friend Alex, I would be forced to report him to his principal. I told them that Tim and Terry would continue to walk their sister and her friend to the bus stop periodically. The subject of replacing the broken glasses fell by the waist side.

CHAPTER 14

THE FOURTEENTH YEAR

It is a new year, but just another lesson that must be learned by my growing twin boys, Tim and Terry. I bought them overcoats at the beginning of this school year. They did not like the coats because they thought them to be too bulky. I told them that they had outgrown all their large winter coats, so this was their replacements. In the dead of winter, Tim and Terry had managed to avoid wearing these new coats until one day. It was ten degrees Fahrenheit on a school morning. I had had enough of this, so it was ultimatum time. I told them to march back into the house and put on their new coats. They complained, saying that they were not cold. I said Ok, this is how this will go down. If you do not wear the coats and get sick, you will owe me. They looked at me like how? I told them that this would fall under the "natural consequence category." I will no longer force you to wear the coats anymore. If you get sick, every dollar I spend, you will owe me. I explained to them that medical bills were expensive, as well as medication prices. I said that any money you get from someone else for your birthday or Christmas would go to me until you are paid in full. Any money you get in any form will go to paying off these bills. They went back in the house, put on their nice new, very warm coats and quietly took off to school with baffling looks on their faces. I do not force everything on them because, at times, there is a lesson to be learned. On another occasion, they did not want to wear these rain suits. I bought them once. They told me that if they wore that, they might get beat up at the bus stop. I dropped that one for obvious reasons. I let them pick their own clothes at our favorite department store (lots of name brands that are marked down).

Great fishing day in the Fox River, near downtown South Elgin. It was the twins, and I just loved every moment of it. Some other fisherman gave us his leftover live bait (Crawfish), and that turned out to be a wonderful thing. We caught a lot of fish, and as usual, we gave them all away to those in need and older people. I always taught the boys the art of catch and release, except if we knew we could help someone in need, we would.

I was waiting for something musical that I could introduce the twins to, and what we decided was drums. A music instructor was found, and she accepted them and rented a complete drum set for practicing at home. Once a week, they came in for lessons at their instructor's studio. The boys were excited and eager to get started. I would estimate that their interest in playing the drums lasted about three weeks. They stopped practicing at home and were not that enthusiastic about going to practice with their instructor. I pulled the plug with little or no resistance from my Percussion enthusiast sons.

On the first day of High School, the twins start their freshman year. They were excited about trying out for the ninth-grade freshman baseball team. I knew this, so I decided to collaborate with them over the upcoming winter at the indoor baseball hitting and fielding range. Every Saturday night, I ended up taking them with their friend Byrd, usually. I let them get adjusted to the high school way of things before I brought up what I expected from them, involving their grades. I explained to them that I would be asking for their current grade average for each of their classes. They were confused by my request. I explained that I expected them to know what their grade was at any point in a semester. I showed them how to get an average from a group of numbers. I told them to keep all their daily grades so that when I asked, all they had to do was average out their grades, and bam, your current grade point average. I refused to accept the I do not know the answer. They did not want me going to their teachers at all (a lesson they learned the hard way in prior school years).

Baseball tryouts had begun, and it was an extremely exciting time for both Tim and Terry, not to mention myself included. I knew how important this was for them. They ended up making the freshman team, and the joy was shared between all three of us. The season started, and I was there for their first game. Tim and Terry sat on the bench the whole game and never played. The thing is, the team got beat badly because of a plethora of mistakes. I mentioned none of this to the boys. I just stayed positive. They knew from years earlier when I nipped that complaining stuff in the butt right in front of them and their coach years earlier. Game two comes and goes just as the first game went, with the twins riding the bench for the entire game. I started asking the boys about the possibility of them not performing in practice, but they said no. I decided to go to one of their practices, and what I saw was kids playing in the game with fewer playing skills than the twins. Tim and Terry had like ten years of baseball experience, and it just bothered me. Game three begins and ends with the twins sitting on the bench the whole game. After the game, I strode over to the coach to ask him if Tim and Terry would be playing anytime soon. The coach said never, which caught me off guard. I immediately informed the coach right then (it was not planned) and there that Tim and Terry would not be returning. I told him that I would be placing them on a little league team where they would be playing a lot, according to their experience of ten years playing baseball. I put them on the Little League senior baseball team. They played a lot and were happy that I got them out of that situation. My sons enjoyed playing baseball again. Turns out that the kids are playing on the freshman team; parents were boosters, case closed and welcome to politics.

Even at the little league level, I got lots of politics from my parents at games. Saying what their kids would be doing next year (tenth grade) at the new South Elgin High School. For instance, I had a conversation with a parent at a baseball game. It was a teammate of the boys, Kenny. Kenny's mom told me that her son would be playing second base for the junior varsity baseball team. Kenny was so bad at playing baseball it was difficult to watch. So, I said how do you know this without tryouts to make the team. She said that Kenny would play no matter what because she would be a booster. There it was, politics strikes again. At another game, another parent (Phil's mom) says to me that her son Phil will be playing in the Major Leagues. Without any hesitation, I said that Tim and Terry would be Major League baseball owners. She was dumbfounded and speechless. She was only able to acknowledge me with a head movement up and down. I had to do it because I was, after all, the spokesperson and advocate for my sons.

Whitney joined a girls' softball team, which took away from my time with Tim and Terry's baseball activities. Turned out to be a good thing for this break. They got into fishing a lot and hung out with friends. They were always on their bikes and seemed to be having a happy life. Whitney, on the other hand, turned out to be a good softball player. It was a great period for her and me to bond. I kept an eye on the boys, but most of my attention was on my daughter.

Whitney's first year playing Softball was an overwhelming success. I knew she was athletic because she would play basketball with her brothers against other boys. She had also played basketball for one year on a coed team and stood out as one of the best players. Whitney's position in Softball was shortstop or third baseman.

She had the strongest throwing arm on the team, as well as being the fastest runner. She threw the kids out effortlessly. Before each game, I would warm Whitney up. It caused a stir because of how hard she and I threw the softball at each other. I truly believe that Whitney could have easily played little league baseball with the boys. Unfortunately, she started her menstrual cycle after that softball season and basically never played again. So, my daughter's sports playing ended before her twelfth birthday.

I feel so blessed to even have had the opportunity to raise three wonderful children. They gave my life purpose and made me take on the task at hand to teach them all the virtues from my life experiences. Parenthood was therapeutic and life-changing for me in a positive way.

I had always wanted to wait before introducing the boys to weightlifting. I even read a lot on this issue, not to start them too early. Every kid is different and can start earlier than others. I thought they were ready at thirteen years old but decided to wait just to be sure. When they were fourteen years old, I gave them reminders that the day would come when I would be bringing them to the gym to lift weights. I signed them up for my gym membership, which was exciting to me personally. I took them on that first night just to show them how it would be and to make them feel comfortable. Then, the big night, day one, starts with weightlifting first, alternating muscle groups on certain days. After weightlifting, it was time to run one mile, which they hated. Then we played basketball before heading home. The main reason I decided to do this for them was to show them the proper way to lift weights. Also, how to work out each muscle group properly with the right techniques. There were times when I had to force them to go, but they usually wanted to get it in. I would allow them to walk a little on our one-mile run at first, just to get them acclimated. I never stopped because they watched everything I did. I knew that I was their role model, and I had to be their inspiration. There was no way I was going to be messing that up.

CHAPTER 15

THE FIFTEENTH YEAR

This was the first year in a decade that the boys were not on a baseball team. It was like the three of us were sort of lost. They played lots of baseball with friends. Pickup games and home run derby, but that was about it, sadly. When possible, I would go and play with them. It did not seem to bother the boys, so I just went with it. Tim had developed into a surprisingly good first baseman, and Terry was good at multiple positions, such as second base and all outfield positions. Terry had a very strong throwing arm and was good with his accuracy. Tim is left-handed, so first base was a natural position for him. The outfield position is another position that Tim could play, but he was lights out at First base. I just think it's just a darn shame how high school baseball is so political. I enjoyed watching and being a part of the years of baseball the twins played. I believe this was a positive life experience and showed them the true meaning of teamwork. They will be able to take that experience far into their adult years.

The first day of school for the tenth grade would mark the last year that the twins would be without a license and a car. Shortly after the start of that school year, they turned fifteen years old. On the day of their birthday, I asked them if they were going to look for jobs. They both told me no. I accepted that, as I said, but they also knew what would be happening once they became sixteen years old, one year from that day. I told the boys that if they declined to work as sixteen-year-olds, I would cut them off. They wanted to know what that meant. It will not be wonderfully comfortable for them as it pertains to all the things they enjoyed just would not be available anymore. I explained to them how I had been working since I was nine years old (cutting people's grass for a profit). How important it was to be a person with a job. They did not seem to care, so I dropped it. They were content with enjoying being unemployed. There was an incident between the boys involving the removal of snow from a neighbor's driveway. Tim and Terry were helping me shovel snow from this driveway. Once done, I decided many times to do a certain neighbor's driveway snow removal because they were elderly. The twins didn't want to help but did so anyway, as if they had a choice. Once done, I asked them if they wanted to go around the neighborhood shoveling off people's driveways for money. They said no and wanted to go back inside to play video games. I even offered to help them just to get them started, but the answer was still no. I explained to them that I would remember this when they asked me for money in the future. Lo and behold, about a couple of weeks later, we were in a store at the Mall Shopping Center. Terry came up to me, like he had done many times before, and asked me if I had five dollars. With no hesitation, I removed my wallet and counted all the money in my wallet. I believe it came out to be eighty-seven dollars. Then I placed the money back into my wallet and returned my wallet back to my pocket. Terry just stood there waiting for an explanation. I said, do you remember that day I asked you and your brother if you wanted to make money removing snow from people's driveways? He put his head down and walked away, knowing that I would not let that go ever (checkmate)! We will see what happens when I ask them about jobs once they turn sixteen years old.

Tim joined the school choir, and I could not ever remember him ever singing. I told him that I was also in the school choir in my high school years. I was enormously proud of him for joining the school choir. It was very enlightening to see him perform in the choir. I would always joke with him that I could hear him, but the girls were very loud. The

Jokester he was when he would just give a passive comment like, "might want to get your hearing checked."

One day, the boys told me that a lot of kids were smoking Marijuana during Physical Education class. They never were interested in drugs, which made my life less chaotic. There were also kids performing sexual acts in the auditorium. One thing about all three of my kids: they told me everything, no matter what. Lying was not accepted in our home, so why not just tell the truth? Keeping things away is the same as lying. Being Catholic, I really kept them on a path of practicing Catholicism. Mass every week and confession on a regular basis. They went to catechism on the regular, with no excuses accepted.

The Summer of Tim and Terry was their greatest to date. They were fifteen years old. There was no baseball or karate during this summer. Not much of anything structured to be obligated, too. They really enjoyed fishing every day. We went camping a lot, which all of the kids just loved.

They played pickup baseball with friends all the time. They got to stay up late, within reason. They got to sleep in and not have to be somewhere. I left them be, except for taking care of the grass cutting and a few other things like laundry.

I would have to reiterate that I, as their father, was never wrong. This kept arguments from happening once I declared this. If I said the sky was green, it was green, even if it looked blue. I would always tell the kids that everything I did was for them. Everything was also for their benefit, no matter how it seemed otherwise. I spent a lot of time explaining myself to them. I remember telling them when I made a mistake (not that I was wrong). I was a Dictator for sure, but only in their best interests. When one of the boys would say, "Well, everyone else is doing it." I would simply say, "If everyone jumped off the house on their heads, would you want to do it too?" That would be the end of that exchange. My children learned that begging did not get them anything. But impressing me by being a good listener or doing well in school would be a lot more persuasive.

CHAPTER 16

THE SIXTEENTH YEAR

Sobridy, my sister's daughter, moved into our home because my sister could only find a small one-bedroom apartment. Sobridy, of course, is also older than Whitney, which was a concern. She was a lot more advanced than Whitney, who was still very innocent by design. This period ended up being a trying one. Sobridy would move into Whitney's room, which was Tim's room, who consequently had to move in with Terry (which was not very accepted by the twins). Trouble started up quickly when I started noticing people staying up too late on school nights. Having a surveillance camera and monitor (with sound) in my bedroom caught all the bad actors. The camera worked great as a deterrent and cut down on most of the violating of my self-imposed curfew rules. What happened was catching Sobridy up goofing off, which got her a night on the floor of my bedroom floor. It was not long before I had to send Sobridy back to live with her mother (my sister Paula).

Driver's education time for Terry and Tim has arrived. They brought home all the information from the driver's ed. They handed it to me as I had instructed them to do. Unbeknownst to the twins, I read everything and informed them what would be expected of them at home. What I would be having them do as part of their driver's education course at home. Terry complained, but Tim never did (that much). The home portion of their driver's education activities was something I was all in on, to a tee! We did everything on their list and more that I added in. I was a Professional Truck Driver, and they knew it would be this way because they knew their father was by the book. They had to drive in the rain, snow, sunshine, overcast days, and at night (and much more).

I had them drive in every weather condition. They drove on the freeway, city streets, country roads and more. We spent time backing and parking from different angles. The first to get a learner's permit was Tim, and shortly after, it was Terry. I had to force Terry since he was not as into driving as Tim was.

The day arrived when Tim and Terry became sixteen years old. When everything settled down, it was time to bring up work. I approached the twins to ask them if they wanted to get a job. They said no again, so without showing any indignation, I told them that they were both "cut off"! I got up and went back upstairs without explaining just what that meant. About a week later, I took Tim, Terry and Sobridy to a high school football game. As we walked up to the ticket booth, all was normal for now. One of the boys' friends (Anthony) was at the ticket booth too. I bought an adult and student (for Sobridy) ticket, and we just walked in to go to our seats to watch the game. The look on Tim and Terry's faces was pure amazement and disbelief. I just told them that you are "cut off" and to enjoy the game from out here. Their friend Anthony paid for their tickets, but I knew they understood their father was not going to bend. The next example of being cut off came at a hamburger restaurant. Keep in mind that prior to them being cut off, I would tell each kiddo to order off the ninety-nine-cent menu and get five items. Well, my three kids and I walked into the restaurant for lunch. I ordered after my daughter Whitney's order was in, then informed the cashier that my order was complete. I explained to the twins that if they wanted hamburgers, I would make some at home. You are cut off. I told them that all the luxuries they once had were no more. I said that I could not give money to someone who did not have a job. Able-bodied people asking for money when they were able to work but decided not to was unethical to me. I am here to show you moral values, and I aim to do just that. The boys seemed unphased.

The last straw came when it was time to purchase the boys' new suits for their first communion ceremony in front of the whole packed church. You should have seen their faces when I pulled into a resale shop to buy them clothes for their first communion (in front of a packed church). Every item they wore for their first communion ceremony was used. It must have been the last straw. I was more stubborn than they were, not to leave out more patience. They sat me down one day to say that they now wanted a job. I explained to them what the rules would be when they got a job. They could not work late on Sunday through Thursday nights. They had to obtain acceptable grades in school. If their grades dropped, they would not be able to work until those grades went back up. Of course, that would mean being "cut off again."

We go to a local Hamburger restaurant on our first stop, and they both get hired on the spot. I was so proud of them. They got their first check and came home to another counseling session. I made them a complete budget, complete with strict rules:

1. You must always have $10.00 in your wallet.

2. Savings were off limits until they got to $500.00 (which would be an emergency account), not to be touched without my approval.

3. If you wanted to make a purchase, you had to save up for it and never take it out of your savings!

4. You will give 10% to church, monthly divided by 4 weeks. 5). Invest in US Saving Bonds.

5. Lastly, invest in yourself. (If I were you, I would save for a possible future car.)

Tim came home from school one day and decided to get on my bad side. He starts off with, now that I am sixteen years old, I can quit school. I started locking doors and windows. This scared him because he started asking what I was doing. I said that I was about to break out a can of wipe ass on him (I was kidding, but he did not know that). He quickly said that he was kidding around. I knew he was because he was doing so well in school, and I knew he loved school. It was a moment between my son and me that I didn't want to be left out of this book. We laugh about it now.

Time for their first vehicles. But not before setting down the rules. I told them that if I had to, I would ground their car. Yes, even if you bought it, take it or leave it. Also, to follow all state and local laws, the big two were curfew and being limited to only one passenger except for siblings or parents. Tim got Grandma's Dodge Caravan Van since she bought her another car. The only problem with the Van was that it burned oil badly (perfect). Tim was educated on how important it was to check the oil daily and add oil as needed (I helped with purchasing oil). Tim was responsible for paying $400.00 for the Van. He would also have to pay for fuel, oil, and maintenance (within reason). He agreed and bought the Van, and became a car owner. Tim also paid a portion of his insurance (an exceedingly small amount; it is the learning to be financially responsible that counts here). In my opinion, kids are more responsible when they must pay for their possessions. You should have seen how this kid took care of his Van, kept his grades up and was a productive citizen.

Terry agreed to all my rules (especially since he was right there when Tim was going through my process) and demanded, just as Tim had earlier. It was different with Terry because we had to purchase his car from a used car lot. He agreed to pay $700.00 to me (I bought the car for $2700.00). Keep in mind that both the car and the Van cost more than the boys paid for them. It was me who was showing the boys a little life experience. It is time to leave the used car lot, so I tell Terry to just follow me home. I enter traffic, making a left turn. Terry never catches up with me, so I pull over on the side of the road and wait. Finally, I drive back, and oh no, Terry is involved in an accident. He was hit while making a left turn. Thank goodness he was not hurt badly, except for a hurt knee. He was also not in the wrong. He refused medical attention and seemed to be okay. The Police officer was about to call for a toll truck. That is when I went into action by pulling out the fender to the officer's liking, and I ended up driving Terry's car home. Kelli arrived, and Tim drove my Truck while Terry was too shaken up to drive. Terry ended up needing Physical Therapy. Thank goodness for it not being more serious.

The boys came up to me to ask if they could work a second job. The way they did it really made me admire them as being more mature. My stipulation was that they maintain their grades and adhere to curfew. So, Terry went on to work at a major department store while continuing at the Hamburger restaurant. Tim got an interview with a Hardware store. I finally talked him into wearing a suit and tie to his interview. They were so impressed with him he was hired on the spot, pending a drug test. I told him that there was something to make a first impression. These two young men had grown up right before my eyes. They went through all my unorthodox style of parenting with excellence. I was extremely impressed with them and their positive attitudes. My whole thing was to turn them into Alpha Males and the leaders of men. The closer they got to going on their own, the more I reminisced about the beginning. People said things as they will never be normal, and the worst things that I heard. I want to thank all those people for doing that for me. It lit a fire under me to prove them wrong.

CHAPTER 17

THE SEVENTEENTH YEAR

First, disciplinary action concerning the boys' young driving experience. The rule broken was to have no friends riding in a vehicle in which they were driving until after their probation period. There was only one exception where a licensed driver was in the car. While driving home from shopping, I noticed the Van (Tim's vehicle) parked next to the river and softball fields. I went to investigate what was going on. Tim and Terry were both there with Anthony, their friend. I asked how Anthony got there, and without hesitation, both of my sons said the truth. Anthony had been riding along with them, a violation of a strict rule, for safety reasons. I was proud of them for telling the truth, but I still had to punish them to deter this from happening again. I told Anthony to go home (walking) and sent Tim and Terry home. Once home, I told them that they were restricted from driving until the next week. They knew it was wrong and the reason the rule was set into place. While at home, I got a call from Anthony's mom. She was upset that I told Anthony to walk home (collateral damage). Tim and Terry walked home, too. I told Anthony's mom what had occurred and that I grounded Tim and Terry from driving for a set period. She still did not like the fact that her son had to walk home. Keep in mind that it is midday with beautiful weather. Anthony was seventeen years old with about five blocks to walk. If he would have asked for a ride, I would have given him one. She handed the phone to her husband, Chris. He understood immediately, and we both agreed it was the right thing to do.

On the twins' seventeenth birthday, I barbecued and invited many of their friends. They were seniors in high school and made me proud every day of their continued development into young men. During the party, after my cooking duties were completed, the adults were all out front having friendly conversations when a friend of the boys came up to me and said that a girl was straddling Terry and grinding with him. Found out later that this was the knucklehead who reported Tim and Terry to the police for paintballing houses. I went to the closed porch and saw nothing of the sort. I explained to Terry and the young lady what this kid had said to me.

They denied it, and I believed my son 100%. It became common knowledge that this kid had done things like this a lot. I told the boys not to invite him again. They did not have a problem with that. Tim and Terry were self-sustaining, meaning they supported themselves to a certain extent. They both were working two jobs simultaneously. They were keeping their grades up without any special help. They had come a long way in the academic part of their development. To the point where the conversation in our house was that they would be going to the local community college. Something that was once told to us that that would never ever happen. They paid for their vehicle's gasoline, oil, car insurance (a percentage), vehicle maintenance, and cell phones, including service. One might say that I was too hard on the twins, having them pay for all of that on their own. The boys got more of a benefit from this way of being raised than the opposite. They learned the value of money and how to operate with a budget. They learned valuable experience of being responsible with bill paying. What they got from this experience will stick with them through their adult years. In my opinion, kids who are given everything without any real-world experiences about just how hard it is out there are the ones who suffer many times. I believe that Tim and Terry will survive in tough times and be real heads of their families in the future. I think their future wives will benefit from all of mine and their arduous work. I have done for them what did not happen for me growing up. I would believe in my heart if I had a father like I am today. Who knows where I would be today?

Tim's van finally died because he did not check the oil like I told him to do (a natural consequence). The engine threw a rod, which destroyed the engine. I found out about this one night with a phone call from Tim saying that his van had broken down. I asked him where the van was located, and he said in the middle of the intersection. Seconds later, I got a call from the local police department. Since the van was in my name, it was my responsibility to oversee it. I called a tow truck and had it towed home. Tim simply left the Van where it broke down and walked the rest of the way to work. Tim was fully employed, so it was no big deal. It was a first for Tim, with a breakdown. I first got apoplectic but quickly got that to an infinitesimal amount. Tim was maudlin, so that was another reason to take it easy on him. He learned his lesson, and I learned to allow these young men to learn through natural consequence. So, Tim and I went out to a used car dealership to look for a replacement car for him. I donated the Van to a charity organization that helped children. I decided to flip a switch and help him in a way that he would not realize until years later. I picked out a car for him that had a five-speed manual transmission. I thought it was an erudite move. Surprisingly, Tim went along with my recommendation (it meant a lot to me that my son trusted his father). So, my son bought the car all on his own. I got a little emotional because of this fact. My boys were going to be fine in this very tumultuous world we live in. Over time, after I taught him how to properly drive his car, he came to love it.

Terry gets into an accident and is taken by ambulance to the hospital with no life-threatening injuries. When I saw his car, it was eerie, to say the least. Through Physical Therapy and pain pills, Terry was able to bounce back to being his old self. What happened was that a truck ran a stop sign at an intersection that did not have four-way stop signs.

We were incredibly lucky he did not get a more serious condition from this accident. So, Terry and I went out to check some used car lots. Finally, he finds a car that he wants. There was no way he would get a car with a manual transmission, no way, Jose. I went through the same natural high as Terry bought his car all on his own, just like Time had done earlier. I was so proud of my son, especially after what he had gone through.

Graduation day has arrived, and I am elated. When the twins were new-borns, no one expected them to ever be where they were on this day. I was so proud of them and, at the same time, happy for them. I thought back to when I first held them in my arms. The first time I looked into their eyes, I cried. That first time, I fell in love with them. I honestly believe that they fell in love with me, too. I knew that they would soon be on their own, and I, at this moment, realized this like a blow to the head.

CHAPTER 18

THE EIGHTEENTH YEAR

The Summer of Tim and Terry's seventeenth year was a major turning point for all of us. The twins were enrolled in community college. Kelli moved out and eventually filed for divorce to end our marriage. I was able to keep them in school financially for the rest of 2007 and some of 2008 before the money was running out towards the end of 2008. All had calmed a bit so we could all recover from a crazy year. Tim and Terry were dealing with things well under the circumstances.

They lost themselves in their school and work. We did not see each other a lot because of our busy schedules. When we did see each other, we enjoyed some quality moments here and there.

One day, I came home with a girlfriend (Laura), and soon after, she moved in. Neither Tim nor Terry liked her, and Whitney, who lived with Kelli, really did not like her. Plus, the fact that both of her daughters also moved into our home. Not long after this period, I got a new dog who was only 6-8 weeks old. I picked him up from the airport. He was an American Bulldog whose name was Rex Amillion. It helped a lot to have a new dog because he kept us all busy.

CHAPTER 19

THE NINETEENTH YEAR

The new year was none eventful, as we all just went through the motions of life. By springtime of 2009, the girlfriend experience was over. Laura moved out, and our house was at peace again. With all three of my children not really liking Laura, it was doomed. It was my fault for bringing a girlfriend into my children's lives so soon after the separation from their mother. I went to our Catholic Diocese and asked for a full annulment from Kelli because I had no intention of living alone. It was an exceptionally lengthy process, but years later, I was awarded a complete Annulment. It was important to me to properly move on.

So, it was time for the enrollment for the spring semester. There was no more money, so a decision had to be made. I sat Tim and Terry down, and we brainstormed about some solutions. Finally, I mentioned the military as a way of getting free college-paid tuition. I set up the computer and showed them the basic training for the Marines Corps, Army, Air Force, and Navy. I showed them the Navy last to not try and impose any influence since I was once in the Navy myself. They both picked the United States Navy and, on their own, went to the US Navy recruiter and started the process of joining the Navy. Tim went to boot camp first, and a few weeks later, Terry went. Before Terry left, I decided to move back to San Diego, California.

We lost Whitney before all of this; we were all hurting badly. I will be dedicating this book to her memory. This will also have lots of pictures. It was a terrible time for us, and we will never get over this period. We went through my drama of bringing home a girlfriend, which was not a good decision. The divorce and subsequent dream of supporting Tim and Terry in getting a college degree ended abruptly.

Getting a new puppy and having to find a place for my mother to live (who lived with us) was tough. Then, seeing Tim and Terry man up and take the initiative on their own by getting into the US Navy was big time. Then, my eventual move back to San Diego.

CHAPTER 20

THE TWENTIETH YEAR

With both Tim and Terry in the Navy, I took off for San Diego, California. Chicago was a life experience, but that time had come to an end. I loaded up my truck on the car carrier, keeping the things I needed while I sold most of the rest in a garage sale. Basically, I gave many things away. It was my dog Rex and I in a moving truck hauling my personal truck on the back. It took two days to get to San Diego. That chapter was over in my life. It was time to start a new one.

After living with a friend for a few months, I ended up renting a home. It was in downtown Chula Vista, California. I would later meet my current wife during this time, eventually getting married, and to this day, we are happily married. I met Claudia Mercedes in a coffee shop and hit it off immediately. Claudia healed my broken heart and restored my confidence. She is the best thing that ever happened to me.

2009 was a year of sorrow, change in perspective, and the new view of life and my future. So in 2010 now that the boys were off in the Navy and focused on their future and their goals, I decided to make some changes and move back to San Diego California. When I made the decision to move, I never realized how quickly things would change in my life for the better. As the cliché saying says, when the door closes, another door or window opens. So on a beautiful sunny afternoon in April, I saw and met someone that would completely change my life and the direction of it. Her name is Claudia and she is a mother of two. We sat down at a coffee shop and chatted for hours on end. I've never met someone like her. She was so full of life so positive and I couldn't take my eyes off of her. She had a golden brown hair, piercing green eyes, and this confident femininity about her that left me breathless. After talking with her for a bit, she drew the line that first she had no intention on getting married again. Secondly, I would not be meeting her children anytime soon and thirdly tonight tell her that I have fallen quickly in love with her, because it would be tempting. The confidence and humor and beauty just continued to intrigue me, and with our conversations I felt I had known her my whole life, and I knew in that moment that my life would change. After a few hours of talking, which only felt like a few minutes time just flew by she graciously said that she had appointments to keep for the afternoon and she needed to get going. I quickly invited her out for a movie or a late lunch or an early dinner but unfortunately she had prior commitments. Later, I would learn that she had done this on purpose to keep me wanting more and it worked. Lol.

Her personality was so magnetic that she continued to draw me in day after day week after week then month after month. We would talk for endless hours on the phone about our goals in life our family, and what direction we saw our lives going in. She talked highly about her family. She comes from Latin descent and was very proud of her culture but most importantly of the unity in her family. After a few weeks of talking, she mentioned to me that she had done a few background checks on me and then she also mentioned that the neighbors across the street were in the police department and Bill had run my license plate since he had seen my truck in the driveway a couple times. The good news is that my background check was clean and Bill had also run and checked everything he could and I came out squeaky clean. This was very important to do since she had two very young children and the next step was me meeting them.

Slowly, but surely, as we continued to get to know each other, we became closer and closer, and she had mentioned that it was scary how easy going it always was when we were together. We would laugh we would talk for endless hours. We simply just enjoyed each other's company, and there was never an issue. No jealousy, no games ,no lies,no disrespect. The fact was that, even though she looked Caucasian, she was of Hispanic and Latin descent, and I was a black man. Something people might find this to be a problem coming from two very different worlds when it came to culture and upbringing. However, for us, it was simply meeting our soulmate. I had finally found my best friend someone who had my back immediately as I had hers. We had both been through a lot in the prior years and have some failed relationships. But our relationship felt like a fairytale something that you could read about in a romance novel. If I could only dream of finding someone that completed me. Neither one of us expected this, and it gave both of us moments of pause and even anxiety at times. Carefully questioning our relationship of really being this easy, and loving. We soon found out that we were simply blessed to have found each other. As we trusted and treasured what we had in each other.

After a few months of courtship, she introduced me to her kids and I didn't expect it to happen so quickly, but everything just fell in line and it felt so right. The kids enjoyed having me around and they called me Mr. Marvin. I really enjoyed the kids calling me that it made me feel special and excepted. We were forming a family with our four children and we were very protective of it not letting other people's opinions, comments or negativity affect us in anyway. We knew what we had was very special and so we were very protective of it and we kept nothing from each other. We always spoke about the good the bad, the ugly and the hilarious, because sometimes the comments that other people would make you couldn't help but laugh. We did not allow that to burst our bubble. On the contrary, it only made us stronger and more united.

I knew from the onset that I wanted my future to be with her and so the next step was to meet the parents. She warned me that, even though she had been married before, and had two children. In her father's eyes, she was still his innocent daughter that needed to be protected. So she mentioned to me that the first question that her father would make would be " young man what are your intentions with my daughter? Proceeded by what are your intentions with my grandchildren?". We meet on a predetermined date at a breakfast style restaurant, for this somewhat grand occasion. Even though she had warned me, I was not prepared and so as I took a sip of coffee, and tried very hard not to spit it out, as I heard the questions that she had warned me about. I looked at him, man-to-man and straight in his eyes, and said my intentions in the future is to marry your daughter, and to be a father figure and positive role model to your grandkids.

The next introductions was for her to meet the twin boys and they both liked her immediately they saw the positive influence that she had on me and how happy she made me. This made me feel so at peace. Now it was Tim, Terry, Cristian and Paulina, with Claudia and I. A truly happy family and in a roundabout way…completeness in my life.

CLAUDIA ALEXANDER

Meeting Marvin was a blessing with the bonus of his twin sons, Tim and Terry. As our relationship evolved, I started looking at Marvin as a second father figure to my children, Cristian and Paulina. It made me reflect on my influence on Tim and Terry. I would have the opportunity to be a bonus mom. Marvin and I have always seen ourselves as parents without the word step. Which means I am blessed to have four children. I remember telling Terry that I would always love him. I may not always like your choices or decisions, but he would always be able to count on me and my love. This was around the time that both Marvin and Terry moved in. Tim and Terry had joined the Navy and were beginning their careers. Terry was stationed in San Diego, while Tim was stationed in Bangor, Washington. The whole family was immensely proud of them serving our country.

Our daughter Paulina was in the Girl Scouts, so when it came time to sell the magical cookies, she also wanted to honor her brothers in the Navy. So, she decided to sell cookies for our servicemen and women in their honor. She did such an amazing job that she was recognized on board the USS Midway for selling the most cookies for our service men and women. Our son Cristian was also so proud and shared that his two brothers were in the US Navy. In the share and tell part of his book report at school.

I remember meeting Tim for the first time since he was in Washington State. I was so nervous about whether he would approve or like me. I was taken by his maturity and how relaxed he was, always enjoying the moments life gave him. I was so proud to see both Tim and Terry standing next to their dad on our wedding day. They were the best men; it was our honor to have them both for our special day. I had been blessed to be able to take Tim shopping for clothes, making sure we got him some nice outfits along with those perfect jeans. Taking him to play Blackjack for the first time at a casino. Talking about religion, relationships, and life. I also introduced him to a little of my Latin side. No matter what we did, it was always so carefree and incredibly special to me, like shopping at Pikes Pier in Seattle, Washington, and him coming up to me with my favorite tulips, just because. He will never know how much that meant to me. Tim was my son from the first moment I met him. He is now a man of conviction, a diligent worker and a lover of nature. He lives life with peace in his heart and a love for life. He is a few years away from completing his twenty years in the US Navy. I cannot wait to see what the next chapters in his life will be. It will be my blessing to be a part of his world.

I remember the moment I met Terry. Marvin was an over-the-road Trucker. I picked up Terry and brought him to their home on Shasta Street in downtown Chula Vista, California. I could see he was a bit nervous, but so was I. Then, he was to report to 32nd Street Naval Station in San Diego, California. I told him not to worry and that I'd wake up early to take him to his first day. At his duty station, I remember dropping him off, and they were calling me his mom, which made me proud. For weeks, Cristian, Paulina and I would wake up early and drive him to his base at 4:30 am. As he would report for duty, I was already being a protective mom. I recall talking with Terry about relationships and taking him on shopping trips to make sure his jeans looked exactly right. Having those priceless moments a mom has with her son. Terry has a passion for photography. He took pictures of his brother Cristian when he was the kicker in High School. Cristian was proud to have his brother taking pictures from the sidelines.

Terry was proud that his brother was the kicker. I remember Marvin and I flying to Maryland to be there for him while he had surgery. I prayed for a successful surgery. During this trip, we were able to see the sights within Washington DC Memorials the White House. Then being there for him in his recovery. Marvin and I flew out to Houston, Texas, to see Terry play baseball with the Navy baseball team. I remember them early on taking Cristian under their wings to show him the game. They have all four played catch more times than I can count. Terry loves to travel, Photography, and baseball. He has been stationed in San Diego, Spain, Japan and currently in NAS Norfolk in Virginia. Cannot wait to see what his future entails.

I am proud to be a mom of four. Tim and Terry have brought love and laughter to my life. May God bless them, and may they both know how much I love them.

Hugs and blessings, love you bunches, bonus mom (Claudia).

DEBBIE FARRAR

I am an avid book reader! Wow, I did not know you were authoring a book. Cool! I would have to write about a tall, dark, and handsome man who stole my little sister's heart and had two handsome twin sons!!!!!

JOSE AND JOSEFINA ESQUER

Marvin, both Pina and I have had little contact with your sons, Tim and Terry. During the last few years, they both have had reliable professional careers in the United States Navy. Terry has concentrated on his girlfriend and baseball activities. Tim has focused more on family life and sporting activities such as boating and fishing. Children sometimes find it difficult to communicate with adult family members until they are over 40 years old. When they start to valve both family and close friends. Marvin, I hope these words have helped since kids do not come with a manual. We hope these few words have helped.

- Warm regards, Mami and Papi.

RYAN BYRD

"I remember meeting Tim and Terry when we were on the same baseball team. Got invited to go to the Batting Cages with them and you. Made a good friendship, and we would also go fishing down at the pond. We would ride bikes or hang out at each other's houses. Also, we would play baseball and practice at the park all the time. We would also play basketball at Tim and Terry's a lot."

ANTHONY MUELLER

Growing up with Tim and Terry was one of the most memorable moments of my life. Having their father, Marvin, take me under his wings and treat me like one of his own was something I will never forget and will be forever grateful for. He always wanted us to try our best and was always collaborating with us on and off the Baseball Field. There were so many memorable moments, and I am forever grateful to be able to call them my brothers and their father my second dad. I will never forget all the basketball on the driveway, baseball practice, camping trips and fishing trips. Always occasionally having the term, "Hang and foot up the ***." They will be like my family no matter how far away we are.

With much love, "Rib"!

ZACK PARKS

When we would go to High School Football games, Tim and Terry would come with their father, Marvin. Sometimes, I would bring my son Jared and my brother Zane. They would just be kids having fun playing and riding their Big Wheels. Tim and Terry were always so polite and respectful to us.

Over the years, from the beginning, I knew them. Just to see how things worked out for them was extraordinary. Watched them become good athletes and great young men. They did everything the right way. They were remarkably close to their dad and my best friend, Marvin. At your wedding to Claudia, it was so easy to hang out with Tim and Terry. They had a maturity I noticed when talking about life with them.

JESSICA CONNOLLY SAWYER

I remember Tim and Terry when they were babies and toddlers. They were funny and nice little boys, "Sweet Boys," always kind and polite. I can remember that they loved hanging with me. I was 6 or 7 years old during the times I was around them.

SHAWNA SHETTLER

"Cute little guys, Terry was so smiley, and Tim was more serious looking."

ERIC BRIDGEWATER

There has never been a better dad, husband and friend than my brother Marvin. I met Marvin twenty-plus years ago while working for the same Trucking company. We enjoyed an Italian dinner together near Allentown, Pennsylvania; our friendship and brotherhood took off. As we stayed connected, he would keep me current on what his kids were up to, and I would keep him current on what my kids were doing. I have watched Tim and Terry turn into fine men because of Marvin. I will forever hold Marvin in my heart as my true brother.

- Eric Bridgewater 2022.

AUTHOR'S NOTES

This is my story, where I will briefly lay out what made me the type of parent I eventually became. In the beginning, I was born and dropped off to live with my grandmother. I would call her mom because that is what she was to me. My birth mother was impregnated by my Aunt's Husband (my uncle and father), which is why I went to live with my grandmother while my siblings lived with my birth mother. I went 50 years without knowing who my father was. He died in 1990 without me ever meeting him as my father. This had an unusually positive influence on me. This meant that by the time I entered fatherhood, I would be ready to devote myself 100% to raising my future children. I got out of Louisiana as quickly as I humanly could by joining the US Navy in 1979 while still in High School. After High School, I left Louisiana for good, never returning to live there again. I came remarkably close to joining the US Marine Corps first but changed my mind at the last minute. I was married at the age of 28 years old to Kelli. I was so serious about becoming a parent that I got out of the Navy in 1990 with untold determination. Tim and Terry were born later that year in September. I was not a perfect parent, and I understand that completely, but I was mentally and physically ready to take on fatherhood. My future children were getting a committed father in every way. I would love to see grandkids someday just to spoil and love them. That will complete me in a way that will make it all come full circle. I want to thank everyone who shared their thoughts and warm words.

I appreciate you all from the bottom of my heart.

UNIMAGINED ODDS
By Marvin Alexander

This is something that I have always wanted to do: authoring a book about this experience because it was the most important period of my life until I met my soulmate, Claudia. Raising my children to be as close as possible to productive, law-abiding citizens was a transformative journey, changing me from the carefree mindset of a sailor to a man with a clear sense of purpose. I gave them all that I had and then some. It was my duty to teach them the right way and to know the difference between right and wrong. Most importantly, to understand that there is no in-between. You are either right or wrong. My love for them is off the charts, and I pray that I have conveyed all of that and more in this book. So that generations of Alexander will hopefully benefit from this book and stories of me long after I am dead and gone. I still must author a book about my life someday. That one will be a Roller Coaster.